* | THE
EUCHARIST
YESTERDAY
AND TODAY | *

| THE EUCHARIST YESTERDAY AND TODAY |

M. BASIL PENNINGTON

CROSSROAD · NEW YORK

1984
The Crossroad Publishing Company
370 Lexington Avenue, New York, N.Y. 10017

Printed in the United States of America

Library of Congress Cataloging in Publication Data

Pennington, M. Basil.
    The Eucharist: yesterday and today.
1. Lord's Supper—Catholic Church. 2. Catholic
Church—Doctrinal and controversial works.
I. Title.
BX2215.2.P43   1983   264'.02036   83-7574
ISBN 0-8245-0602-2

To
SISTER M. DE SALES, O.S.B.
and the
BENEDICTINE SISTERS
OF PERPETUAL ADORATION
with affection and gratitude

CONTENTS

✤ ✤ ✤

INTRODUCTION

❀ ❀ ❀

This book is for you, though I must confess that what actually moved me to get started on it was a need to nourish my own priestly and Eucharistic life. In speaking of sacred reading. I have often said that there are three kinds of reading we need to nourish our lives: *sacred study*, to keep our faith culture abreast with our secular culture and to enspirit it so that we, as just persons, can live by faith; *lectio divina*, a faithful and loving listening to the Lord revealing himself to us so that we can experience ever more deeply his love for us; and *motivational reading*. The latter can be quite general, encouraging us to live according to the fullness of the reality of our Christed person; or it can be more particular, responding to a need of the moment such as, for example, a struggle with prayer, a need for forgiveness, or the problem of the Mass losing its meaning.

This last example was my situation. I needed to do some good motivational reading on the Mass. But when I searched for a book on the Mass I found none that seemed to help. So I decided to write one. They say the best way to learn is to teach. Maybe the best way to read, at least to do the motivational kind of reading, is to write. It has helped me, and it has been an enjoyable experience. I hope it will help you too.

Because this volume is intended for sacred reading, I have included in it the texts of a number of Eucharistic prayers, some of which are not readily available elsewhere, so that the reader can, through meditating on them, more fully enter into the heart of the Eucharistic sacrifice.

Many of us greatly regret the loss not only of the sublime beauty and order that marked our liturgical past but even of the assurance of correctness that precise rubrics gave us. Perhaps without our realizing it a bit of the pharisaical spirit had crept in: a sense that God would be pleased if we got the ritual done to the letter, even though we might be neglectful of some of the more important inner dispositions.

Today's evolving and freer liturgical situation is a difficult one, but this difficulty can be seen as an exciting challenge. As a living community, we are responsible to create here and now an expression of our deepest selves in relation to each other, and together, to God our Father in Christ, in his supreme act of sacrificial love. Our liturgy is to be an expression that is adequate, satisfying, and beautiful. We know we will never fully succeed (can we honestly say that the old liturgy actually fully succeeded?), but we can experience ourselves being called forth to live dynamically in the ongoing effort.

Perhaps one of the reasons why we fall back from entering fully into the challenge of the Eucharistic celebration is because it is too painful. It confronts us powerfully with our incompleteness. We stand convicted as persons who have not appropriated the risen life we have acquired in baptism, or as communities still very fragmented because we have not taken on the *mind of Christ*. In the challenge of the Eucharistic celebration we need to look more at the hope and promise of the community in the making than at what is lacking or what could have been. If we are prone to judge ourselves harshly it is because we fail to accept the mystery of sin and grace, the mystery of an unfolding, evolving creation. We tend to want something that is complete once and for all. But the school of growth and love is found in the challenge of bringing imperfection toward perfection.

This is the true nature of tradition. We are challenged to be in the tradition of the Eucharistic. Tradition involves receiving the heritage as fully as we can into the fabric of our actual lives, letting it be formed by our living experience, and then handing it on as a living reality to those coming after us. That is why in this study I have sought both to bring forth in a living way the heritage of the past and to suggest ways in which this heritage can be lived today. The heritage is not to be held as something outside ourselves, an inert treasure. It is to be enfleshed in us, to find new life in us, and thus to be handed on to the next generation as something living and life giving. Our young people do not want to receive from us a codified mummy. But liturgy that is an expression of our true life and woven into it as a bright and sustaining thread will be gratefully received by them.

In these few pages I am certainly not trying to say all that can be said about the Mass. There are many thoughts here that could be much more fully developed. The number of practical suggestions given is very limited. I could easily fill another volume with possible implementations. And so could you. And that is what I want. I want to encourage individual readers, lay and clerical, liturgical teams and parish groups, to look again into Scripture and tradition, into theology and ritual, into the past and the present; to look at the signs of the times and at our hopes for the future, and creatively collaborate to bring into being a communal liturgy that truly celebrates Christian life, that feeds it and satisfies its deepest needs to be uplifting of the world today, as yesterday, and into tomorrow, for the joy of us all, and unto the glory of the Father in the Son through the Holy Spirit.

New wine, rich with promise, can only burst old skins. A new wine of the Spirit is breaking out of the bonds of our ecclesiastical past and enlivening the whole of humanity through a Church that is not a confining old sack, but a gushing source of life and love for every woman, child, and man on the face of the earth. At the very heart of that source from which all flows is the Supper, Calvary, the Mass, our Eucharist, ever old, ever new, the absolute pinnacle of creation's love, the one bonded love that we all are in Christ, the Risen One.

Our Jewish sisters and brothers have been keeping the Holocaust very much before our consciousness. We can at times be tempted to resent this, noting the death of as many gentiles, of as many Christians. But we should be grateful for this effort on the part of our brethren. It powerfully confronts us with the human being's inhumanity toward his fellow humans. Indeed, it challenges our very concept of God. How do we worship a God who allows such monstrous inhumanity to prevail among his creatures? It forces us to go beyond the logical, the philosophical, even the metaphysical, to the mystery, the mystery of Calvary: a God not only permitting, but willing the excruciating death of his own beloved Son as a proclamation of selfless love and the way to glory. Only from the heart of the paschal mystery, which is in foretype at the heart of Judaism, can we understand all the holocausts, great and small, and the often more pressing mystery of the death of one very close, and even our own death—yes, even the possibility of the nuclear annihilation of the human family. If the Mass can give meaning, can give hope beyond hope, beyond our humanly created hells, it can also give hope that we can stop creating human hells. Christ on the cross has assumed all human evil and sin, consumed it, buried it in hell, and has risen to freedom. We don't need to go on creating hell on earth as the fruit of our sin. By the power of the cross, present and available in the Mass, we can *now* rise to a new life, a life of human community, of solidarity in the love of the Spirit poured out, the Spirit who is ours.

I have long wanted to write a book on the Eucharist to pay tribute to two very special persons. The first is Dom Edmund Futterer, my first abbot. The Eucharist was central in my life before becoming a monk. He showed me how it could be central in my life as a monk. The very way he designed and built our abbey church proclaims this centrality. He himself prepared me for my first Mass, after inspiring me for years by the way he himself celebrated the Holy Mysteries. Since that day in 1957 when I first offered Mass as a priest, I have considered it a daily privilege and responsibility to be with Christ in the ministering of his saving passion. It was an occasion of special joy for me recently when many loved ones and friends gathered to help me thank God for twenty-five years of priestly ministry.

I want also to pay tribute to another Eucharistic life, one quite hidden: that of a wonderful little sister, a Benedictine of Perpetual Adoration (who is that in reality and not just in name). Sister Mary de Sales has typed the pages of this book as of so many others for me. Her prayer and wise editorial advice have nourished and enriched them all. (For some years Sister was the editor of a devotional monthly.) But above all, her wonderful witness of the love, joy, and goodness that flows from a Eucharistic life have constantly inspired and uplifted me. Only the recording angels can tell how many thousands of holy hours this Jubilarian has offered to our Eucharistic Lord for us all, how many holy Masses have been truly lived. It is a joy to dedicate this little effort to her.

As I was writing this volume I was also thinking of a Jewish friend whose Irish lover has begun taking her to Mass. Her spiritual sensitivity enabled her to touch something deep in the mystery of faith. She wanted to know more. I hope this book will help her to understand a bit more what we Catholics are about when we gather for Eucharist. We do have so much for which to be grateful!

Before concluding I want to express a public word of gratitude to my abbot and my community. They are the supportive center that makes all that I do possible. It is with them that I most joyfully offer the Mass, finding it ever old and ever new, the great sacrament of our communion of love.

COMING TOGETHER

A Sunday calm rests over the little Greek village in the heart of Halkidiki. A few shutters have been opened to welcome the early morning sun, but the weekday busyness is absent. We have to look in the area of the *katholicon*, the village church, to see any activity. There the elderly pastor is opening the large doors of the narthex. Pigeons scatter from their roosts under the porch shed and a lazy cat moves out from its comfortable corner.

The heavy doors are open now to welcome the people. The priest shoulders his semantron—a board some eight feet long and a half-dozen inches wide—and takes up his wooden mallet. The quiet of the village reverberates with its rhythmic beat. Doors open and children emerge; a procession forms and grows as the pastor makes his way along the village streets past the homes of the people. By the time the shepherd leads the troop of his little ones down the main street directly toward the large open doors of the church, their elders are flocking in from all directions, joining the procession. The pastor is leading the people of God toward the house of God.

A few hundred miles away, on another day and in a very different setting, a Supreme Pastor walks in the midst of a portion of his flock, gathering them, too, to the house of the Lord, re-enacting a scene with centuries of history. It is Ash Wednesday, 1960, and we are on the Aventine, one of the seven hills of Rome. Good Pope John, John XXIII, has come to be with his people for the opening of the Lenten season. Following the tradition, they have gathered at the Church of San Eleseo, and now they make their way slowly through the crowded streets to the beautiful fourth-century basilica of Santa Sabina, a few hundred yards away. The bells ring out a glad summons. The people sing their hymns; soon they will chant their litanies.

It is the gathering of the people of God, the important initial act of the communal worship of the people of God. It is important because, like the whole of the liturgy, it is a sacramental act, signifying inner and transcendent realities.

In its strictest sense a sacrament is an outward sign instituted by Christ to give grace. The Eucharist, surrounded by the other sacraments instituted by Christ, is at the heart of all liturgy. The Church, the people of Christ, following his example and inspired by the revealing activity of the Father under the old dispensation, has in its turn instituted a rich sacramental liturgy in which to set Christ's precious gifts, much like the way a guild of dedicated goldsmiths might create a rich, intricate setting for a collection of precious gems given to them by a great king. The setting itself can be a thing of great beauty, perhaps of great antiquity, with the labor of many lovers having contributed rich inspiration. In itself it can have immense value and say a great deal to us. But it remains ever subordinate to the gems and, above all, to the central gem. As a setting, its whole purpose is to set off the gems so that we can appreciate them more and respond better to their essential beauty.

If we do take the time to study different facets of a rich setting, we must never lose sight of its fundamental purpose. If worship is going to be integral and authentic, the elaboration of the various parts must always be kept in balance and in harmony and be viewed with regard to their purpose as a setting for the Eucharist.

The Eucharist is a *memoria*, a sacramental memorial, not only a calling to mind but a making present of the passion, death, resurrection, and ascension of our Lord Jesus Christ. We tend to consider and to experience events as following one another like so many cars in the train of time, so many posts along the side of the road, so many vistas that present themselves as the human family moves along the highway of life. But in the eternal "now" of God it is not that way. Everything simply *is*, is now, is present. If we were to try to express this graphically we might say that we see things stretching out along a road whereas God sees them all piled up in one column. But whether we conceive all human activity as spread out along the route of history or as drawn together in a "now," the focus of all that goes before and comes after, the apex of the column, is the same. It is that supreme act of love (for God *is* love) whereby the greatest thing in creation—his own human life—was offered to God by God when God entered into our created time. And the Eucharist, the ritual act, the sacrament given to us by God, repeatedly reaches into the eternal "now" and makes that unique, supreme act present in our passing time.

As the supreme act of all creation, Christ's Passover draws to itself all else in creation: *If the Son of God be lifted up, he will draw all things unto himself.* It is a gathering act, a unifying act, the act that makes us one in love and in the realization of our participated being. *That they may be one, Father, as you in me and I in you, that they may be one in us.* The Mass, the Eucharist, is the ultimate coming together of the people of God made present now in our time. The people of God seek to make themselves more aware of this coming together, this "becoming one," by making it sacramentally present in the entrance procession—the coming together of that portion of the people who are now to celebrate the Eucharistic reality.

Our coming together is a response to a call, a call rooted in the creative act that summoned us from nonbeing to being and made us according to the image of the Creator. We were made to his image, in his likeness, so that we could be one with him not only in shared being but in the bonding of mutual knowledge and love. This call was expressed much more personally when we were drawn down into the waters to die with Christ, the Son, so that we might rise up with him to share forever his risen life. A call expressed repeatedly in the urgings of grace, the sharing of faith, the words of Revelation. A call that echoes in the village in the rhythmic beat of the semantron, and in the city, in the peal of bells, great and small.

It is fitting that the divine call to gather, to Eucharist, has its sacramental expression. Every liturgy should begin with the summons of a bell. The gathering bell will not only summon those who can gather physically. It will also invite those who cannot come to send their hearts. It will remind all that they are called, called by a God of love, that they are loved and wanted, that they have the dignity of one who is wanted, wanted even by a God. If we have ears to hear, the church bell can be for us a great cause of joy, a cause for hope, a reminder of our significance which is more than human. Every Christian community owes to itself to have a bell, at least one if not several, a bell that is regularly used. It owes it to itself, and to all who are physically, if not sacramentally, enfolded in its love. These latter may not yet hear its sound as sacramental, but faith does come through hearing. The bell does invite them to have faith, to gather, to recognize and experience their place in the Eucharist.

The Mass begins with a call and a gathering. And the people do gather. A formal procession through the streets, as in the village of Halkidiki or on the Aventine, may rarely, if ever, be possible. But it may be more possible than we might first imagine, and a very meaningful event for a community on Easter night, a patronal feast, or other occasions.

Each time there is a Eucharist, people, his people, gather. As you move toward the church or chapel, whether you are on foot or in a car or bus, it would be well to be aware of what you are doing, to be reflective and share this reflection with others. You are being called and you are responding, you are a people and you are gathering—you are not just going to church or fulfilling a duty. The cars following one another into the parking lot, perhaps with a slowness that demands much patience, are a procession. If you see it in this way, what has been a matter of routine or a trial becomes a moment of grace, a real part of our communal worship.

We can sacramentalize the ordinary and let it speak to us. As a Christian people we want also to create sacraments, rituals, that can speak to us. If the natural flow of the people into the church speaks of our gathering, it is still good to have an entrance procession that explicitly calls us to a reflective awareness that we are a gathered people.

The entrance of the president of the assembly, the celebrant, should always be a significant act. But he should not come alone. He is the president of a people, a shepherd with a flock. Others who will be ministering with him quite naturally should be with him as he enters into the ministry: readers, commentator, acolytes, wardens or ushers, musicians, Eucharistic ministers, deacons and concelebrants, if there be any. But there should be some representation of the people: singers, the choir, those who will bring the gifts and make the petitions, those who prepared the altar and flowers, those who provided the stipend or for whom the Mass is especially offered, and some of the old and the young, the poor and the disabled. *Let my people come.* It may take a bit of effort to gather and organize a significant entrance procession. This effort itself can be sacramental and meaningful ministry, a way of involving others, perhaps some of our neglected young adults. It may also help to fill up some of the front pews.

Even if the entrance procession involves only a small group—or *especially* if the entrance procession involves only a small group—we want to give it enough time to have an impact. It should pass through the midst of the people, in so far as possible, so that they can be drawn up into its movement. And the movement should have a certain dignity about it—even splendor, on due occasions—so that it does not seem merely a necessary or, worse, a hurried getting from place to place. The entrance should be done with enough significance so that it can speak and with enough time so that it can be heard.

Music can play a big part in all of this and the words set to the music can be the interpretation of what is going on. Entrance hymns should be chosen to speak explicitly or implicitly of the gathering. They may well speak of the particular occasion or feast the community is gathering to celebrate, but the idea of gathering should not be wholly absent. In its cupboard the Church has a rich repertoire of traditional entrance pieces called introits. These usually consist of a relatively brief antiphon that sets the tone of the gathering. *Gaudeamus*—"Let us rejoice on the glorious Assumption of the Blessed Virgin Mary, praising God together with all the holy angels." This is sung first by the cantor and then repeated by the community, who repeat it again and again as the cantor sings appropriate verses from the Psalms, and finally a *Gloria Patri*: "Glory be to the Father, the Son, and the Holy Spirit, as it was in the beginning, is now, and ever shall be." Such a simple and meaningful way to let music and word gather us is certainly not passé.

The entrance rite is a sacrament of Christ gathering us all into the oneness of God through the Eucharist. It is a sacrament of our gathering as a people. It is also a call to us to gather ourselves interiorly so that we can worship with our whole mind, our whole heart, our whole soul, and all our strength. The personal and interior dimension of gathering is important and should not be neglected. Otherwise the exterior could end up being only an empty sign rather than a true sacrament. We come to the gathering with our many cares and fears, hopes and desires, from the full activity of everyday life. All of this should not be left behind. It is the stuff out of which our offering with Christ's offering is made. But it all needs to be gathered together. This is one of the fundamental labors of our lives— integration. It is dispersion that saps our lives and destroys us. It is the undue autonomy of certain aspirations that sidetracks us and even turns us from our true goal.

In the Eucharist we have a powerful force—an infinitely powerful force to draw together, heal, and integrate our dispersed thoughts and desires, energies and projects. The sacramental, ritual gathering invites us to begin to open ourselves to and cooperate with the grace of unification. Again, we see here the importance of a sufficiently spacious entrance rite so that the call to gather oneself can be heard and can receive an immediate response. Then we, as individuals as well as a community, will be ready to present ourselves before the Lord.

OUR FAMILY HOME

✣ ✣ ✣

One of the more amusing passages in Scripture for me is in the twelfth chapter of Acts. Peter has just been miraculously freed from prison by an angel. It is still dark, but Peter is eager to get off the streets into some safe place before he runs into the night patrol. He hurries to the home of John Mark and pounds on the outer courtyard door knowing that some of the brethern are keeping vigil within. Finally his pounding is heard and Rhoda, a fearful servant, responds through the closed door. She can hardly believe what she hears, and, instead of opening the door to the anxious apostle, she runs back inside to tell the others, leaving him standing in the street. Knowing the impetuous Peter as we do from the Gospels, we can imagine his reaction. After more pounding he finally got in.

Early Christians gathered in private homes to worship. One had to knock to get in, one had to be recognized as one of the chosen family of God. It was some time before freedom came and Christ was, as it were, at home in this world, and his family had its own home and the door stood open. When we go to church, we do not have to knock on the door. It is our home. We belong to the family of God. We freely enter in. And we should feel ourselves at home. Anglo-Saxons have tended to be a little stuffy about this; Latins seem to have more of a sense of being at home in the house of their Father. We have to accept our own mores and not discomfort others by rudely brushing them aside. But still we can cultivate a good sense of our church as our family home.

Next time you go to church take time to look around and really enjoy it. A couple of years ago I invited a Jewish friend to attend a talk I was giving in the Brooklyn cathedral. When I arrived about a half hour before the talk the cathedral was already quite full. And there was my friend with his five-year-old son. It was the first time they had been in a Catholic church and they were in the main aisle taking it all in. As they walked along, Ben pointed out each thing to little David and they talked about it. It was "my" church, and my friend, visiting it at my invitation, felt free to enjoy it fully with his son. I was happy for them and I could see that many others were enjoying their enjoyment of our cathedral. It is too bad that many of us were first introduced to church as a place where we had to sit still, keep quiet, and struggle with our own boredom, instead of as our family home where we could look around and enjoy all the beautiful things that our family had gathered there for us to enjoy. So, if you have never done it, why not go to church a little early next time and really take a look around your home. It will be a lot more fun if you do it through the eyes of a little one.

When we arrive in church there will undoubtedly be some there praying or meditating. We want to be respectful of them and their need for a certain quietness. But that doesn't mean we have to ignore everyone. If one is obviously engaged with God in prayer we shouldn't butt in on the conversation. But as others are just arriving, taking a seat, relaxing, or gathering their material for the celebration, there is room for a quiet greeting, a handshake, a nod, a smile, an embrace, or a kiss—whatever is appropriate in each case. It is a family gathering in our home. We are all brothers and sisters, children of the one Father, albeit an enormous family and therefore enjoying varying degrees of intimacy. But no one should be treated as a complete stranger.

It certainly would be an incorrect attitude if we conceive of our Lord as some autocratic despot, imperially enthroned in the sanctuary, who wanted all attention to be constantly riveted on him. He made us to be happy, happy with him, to share his happiness. He is happy having us in his and our home. He enjoys us and wants us to enjoy each other. He identifies with us: Whatever you do to the least of the brothers and sisters you do to me. As I greet those around me I greet him.

The focus in church is, of course, the sanctuary, and in particular the altar. The sacramental presence of Christ in the Eucharist in a tabernacle on the altar tends to emphasize this, although there is a growing tendency in our time to return to the older practice of reserving the Eucharist elsewhere. The altar in itself is a powerful sacramental presence of Christ. It is marked with five crosses. When an altar is solemnly consecrated, the bishop very dramatically lights a fire on each of these crosses to proclaim the power of the love of Christ, expressed in his cross and in his five wounds, to enlighten and inflame our hearts and lives. Within the altar are placed what we call relics, some tiny particles from the bodies of saints, some of our brothers and sisters who have gone before us and have done a good job at what we want to do. Often their pictures or statues are around the house, too. All of this reminds us of them, gives us a strong sense of their abiding presence, as do the pictures and keepsakes of loved ones in our homes. For decades after his death, my mother kept Dad's pipes in their place on the mantle. They were precious "relics," and we took comfort in their presence. We knew that, in some very real way, he was never gone from us.

The altar is focal, too, because it is the dining table in the family home. And the meal, sharing food, is very much at the heart of most family gatherings and celebrations. Jesus seems to love parties and meals. So often he described heaven as a big feast, as something very special, like a wedding. And how often during the few years of his public ministry do we find him enjoying a meal, a feast. His first miracle was at a wedding feast. When he called Matthew to discipleship or Zaccheus to conversion, he was soon in their homes enjoying their friends and their food and drink. The more pious were somewhat taken aback, even as some are in our churches today when they see others really enjoying the liturgy. We do speak of the celebration of the Mass. *Let's celebrate!*

Singing is a big part of celebration. What is a party, a family gathering, without singing? When I was a boy, in the days before television invaded the family sanctuaries, our family used to gather regularly on Sundays. In the summer afternoons there would be tennis, in the winter, Monopoly. Then Grandma would lay out the traditional Sunday-night supper: baked beans and apple sauce, with apple-sauce cake. After the dishes were cleared away, we would all gather around the piano. I was always amazed the way Uncle Joe, who played by ear, would run his fingers from one end of the keyboard to the other. And we sang all the old favorites. Singing was the climax of our family being together. There, in song, we were most together. Whatever we were singing, we were really singing of our love for each other and our joy in being together.

Jesus loved song and music. With his Father, in planning the Temple liturgy, he made ample provision for musicians and singers. He inspired King David to compose beautiful songs and called forth Solomon's Song of Songs. At his birth his Father provided angelic choirs. As a boy and young man he sang and danced in the synagogue at Nazareth, at the Temple in Jerusalem, at wedding feasts. At the first Mass, he and his disciples sang the familiar Hallel. "Sing to the Lord," he says to us again and again in the Scriptures. When we relax, forget ourselves, and join in the singing, our hearts soon begin to warm. We know a real oneness with others when our voices rise together in a common song. And our devotion and participation in the celebration become very real and really enjoyable. As Saint Augustine said, "One who sings, prays twice,"—and is apt to pray twice as well, because more of the person is in it. And we will enjoy it more. "Sing to the Lord a new song." Alleluia.

Before discussing further the celebration itself, let's take another look around the place of our celebration, our church, our family home—ours. It is ours and we should enjoy it, take pride in it, make it a beautiful place for ourselves, for others, for our God and Father. The many prescriptions he gave to the children of Abraham when they were building his first home on earth shows he does care about the beauty of his house. Today we use our God-given talents and initiative to do something beautiful for God.

Some years ago Malcolm Muggeridge wrote a book entitled *Something Beautiful for God*. It was about Mother Teresa. She had described her life as an attempt to "do something beautiful for God." And she has succeeded. By being so responsive to God's grace and love and by reflecting that love to others she herself has become one of the most beautiful persons in this world of ours. She has also done beautiful things for thousands and thousands of his poorest and most abandoned—I should say, *our* poorest and most abandoned. They all are our brothers and sisters. People come first. They—we—are God's primary dwelling place here on earth.

Do you remember that scene at the opening of Saint John's Gospel? In those days as in ours young men were looking for guides, for teachers, for masters who could show them the way to the fullest meaning of life. Andrew and John had left their home town of Capernaum on the shores of the Sea of Galilee and had trekked south to the banks of the Jordan. They had heard that a prophet had come from the desert and was teaching there. Maybe he had the answers. "No, I am not the one. There is one who is coming after me," said John the Baptizer. Then one day he looked over the heads of his disciples and cried: "Look, there is the Lamb of God." John and Andrew heard what he said and headed off after Jesus. Jesus turned to them and said—as he is saying always to each one of us—"What do you want?" John knew what he wanted; he wanted to stay with someone who had the answers. "Master, where do you dwell?" Jesus answered, "Come and see." John and Andrew did. They followed Jesus, and it was a long road before they got their answer. It was perhaps three years later when Jesus finally said, "If anyone keeps my commandments, the Father and I will come and we will take up our *dwelling* in him." Jesus'—God's—favorite dwelling place is in us, in human persons. Our first care should be for human beings, for ourselves and others. If we are going to do something beautiful for God, we should first seek to become beautiful ourselves by being a complete "yes" to God and doing beautiful things for others.

But there is room in our lives to do something beautiful for God by making our church a beautiful place for God and for all of us, his family. Each of us has talents and skills, whether it be plumbing, carpentry, painting and designing, sewing, arranging flowers, or sweeping and scrubbing. We each can do something to make God's house more beautiful. Unfortunately, we sometimes suffer some frustration in this area. We want to do something, but the community leadership, be it the priests or others, wants us only to pray and pay while they take care of things their way. True, there is need for some money for supplies and such, and not everyone can be in on every decision. But those in leadership should take care that everyone in the family has an opportunity to make a contribution, according to each one's talents, to beautify and care for our churches. Local talent, before all others, should be employed. It is *our* home, *our Father's* house.

Let us together make it a beautiful place to come together to worship, to celebrate. Here is where we come together to share our common story. Here is where we recall our common covenant. Here is where we drink and eat together. Here is where we come together as a family—the family of God—gathered in our family home in joy.

PURIFY ME, O LORD

✠ ✠ ✠

Haec nox est!
("This is the night!")

This is the night when first you saved our fathers: You
    freed the people of Israel from their slavery and led
    them dry-shod through the sea.

This is the night when the pillar of fire
    destroyed the darkness of sin!

This is the night when Christians everywhere, washed
    clean from sin and freed from all defilement, are
    restored to grace and grow together in holiness.

The night is not dark, the moon is full. Small groups converge from all
directions, no one is alone, each has his or her sponsor. It is Easter night
and the faithful are gathering with their bishop, the Pope of Rome, at the
patriarchal church of Saint John Lateran. But as they approach, the Constantinian basilica stands dark, its great door still tightly closed. The
faithful direct their steps to the octagonal building that stands at the
eastern end of the plaza. It is the baptistry.

On this night those who have patiently walked the way of catechumens
during the long penitential season are to enter fully into the passion, death,
and resurrection of Christ the Lord, are to enter the Church as full members of her communion. They have received the creed; they have learned
the Our Father. They have heard the Good News and have welcomed it.
They have been called into communion and are responding. They have
passed through all the stages of the catechumenate. Tonight they enter
the octagonal building. They listen to the final admonition of the bishop.
With him they descend the steps leading down into the large basin of
water in the middle of the building. "I baptize you in the name of the
Father and of the Son and of the Holy Spirit." They go down under the
water, entombed with Christ. They are lifted up, rising with Christ.
They are placed in the loving hands of their sponsors and clothed in

white. A lighted taper is placed in their hands. And, led by the great paschal candle, one with all the faithful, they enter the basilica. They have entered the Church, they are risen with Christ. They are part of the people of God, members of the holy assembly.

Each time we enter the church we dip our hands in the holy-water font and sign ourselves, again washed "in the name of the Father and of the Son and of the Holy Spirit." The graces of baptism are renewed in us each time we enter the church and symbolically proclaim our membership in the holy assembly. In the renewal, many churches have located the baptismal font at the entrance of the church—sometimes the holy-water font is in some way incorporated into it—to help us more fully understand and express what we are doing.

We find our way to a pew, to our place among the people of God. These are not strangers even though we may not know any by name. Of course, if we do know some, or if we are fortunate to be in a gathering where we are all friends, our greeting should be warm and joyful. But even among our unknown brothers and sisters, friendly nods and smiles are not out of place. We belong to each other, we are very much one in Christ. Let us not be afraid to show it. We don't want to be boisterous or barge in on someone who is praying quietly. But discreet, warm greetings, handshakes, hugs or smiles are not irreverent to the Lord in our midst, but are a joy to him. He told us to love one another, and especially to welcome the stranger. Let life and love flow.

On Sunday, the day of resurrection, once we are gathered the priest will often bless water and sprinkle us—another expression of the baptismal reality. We can recall the great Paschal Vigil, on Easter night itself, when baptismal waters were solemnly blessed and new members were brought through the waters into the gathering of God's people, and we all renewed our renunciation of Satan and our commitment to Christ.

As I have noted before, among our Eastern Christian brothers and sisters, at the time of the liturgy there is a gathering in the narthex of the church. This is their place of preparation. Before each principal office, an office of preparation is celebrated there: the midnight office before Orthros (Lauds, or morning prayer); Prime, Terce, or Sext before Eucharistic liturgy; and None before Vespers (evening prayer). This is their place of baptisms, and the place where, before the icons, the spiritual father hears the confessions of his people and absolves them.

When we gather as God's people we need to ask ourselves: What is it we want to happen? What do we need to do to make it happen?

We who are sinners and the offspring of sinners have presented ourselves before the Lord. Our first need is to humble ourselves and be purified. Before God's chosen people could encounter him on Sinai and enter into covenant with him, they had to be delivered from their bondage and be led through the saving waters of the Red Sea. Only then could they be ready as a free people to assent to God's great overture. As we gather, it is to encounter the living God in Christ our Redeemer, and to enter sacramentally into the New Covenant, the covenant in his blood.

In the recent past, when the altar was raised by a series of steps and surrounded by statues of angels and saints, and the air was filled with the mystic strains of Latin Gregorian chant, and the priest ascended amid clouds of incense, signs and symbols carried us into the awesomeness of what we were about. Now the scene is a bit more prosaic, certainly more down to earth. Yet our need to be purified before God remains very much the same. Hence, each Eucharist begins with a preparatory rite that involves purification and conversion. The renewal of our essential purification in baptism, through the use of holy water, is a very significant and appropriate way to express this. In the new Eucharistic rites approved for India, water is used at every liturgy. The option of using water in some way in the opening rite is always available in our Western liturgy, too. It should be used whenever it would be appropriate.

It used to be a fairly widespread custom among Roman Catholics to purify themselves through confession before receiving Holy Communion. With a return to the practice of frequent Communion—and since the Second Vatican Council, with an almost universal return to the early Christian practice of receiving Communion whenever we actively take part in the Eucharist—this custom has been largely abandoned. It is still in fairly rigorous practice among our Orthodox brothers and sisters. Now the reintroduction of a penitential rite into the Eucharistic liturgy makes it possible for this custom to be practiced in a different but effective and meaningful way, reminding us of the traditional teaching that taking holy water, praying the *confiteor* (the general prayer of confession), and receiving the general absolution of the priest, or any one of these, is, for the contrite, adequate for the remission of all lesser sins.

The missal allows the penitential rite to be combined with the litanies that follow. The litanies in the Western rite have been so abbreviated that their absorption into the penitential rite is probably no great loss. But in the East, with the rites of Saint John Chrysostom and Saint Basil, these two elements have remained distinct. As I have mentioned, the penitential preparation takes place in a separate place and with a separate office. The Eucharistic liturgy itself begins with a full litany, concluding with the priestly prayer. Our ritual allows for a very full litany; the petitions can be said or sung by a deacon or a lector, and all the faithful repeat again and again, *Kyrie eleison, Christe eleison, Kyrie eleison*— "Lord, have mercy; Christ, have mercy; Lord, have mercy."

(The Latin Church always retained the Greek language here as a reminder of her universality and the path of her living tradition. It might be a good thing, at least on more solemn occasions, to use a bit of Greek and Latin in our parochial liturgy—in Rome, even lessons are read in Greek on the great feasts. Everyone, with a bit of instruction, can understand *Kyrie eleison*. We tend in many ways to become very provincial, even in these days of mass media and the global village. The effort to express ourselves in the languages of other times and peoples can help us to keep a lively awareness that we do belong to a catholic church; we are heirs of a great living tradition.)

Even if a need for brevity or simplicity calls us to keep this preparatory rite within circumscribed limits, the celebrant should take care that it remains a real call to *metanoia*, a moment of conversion, of baptismal renewal. In the enthusiasm of a great feast, the emphasis may be on the terminus, entering into participation in the effects of the resurrection with the blessed, but it is still a calling forth from wherever we are into a fuller state or presence—in some way leaving behind the bonding or sluggishness of sin, becoming more fully responsive to the communal call to life. A perfunctory reading of the suggestive texts in the missal is hardly adequate. These texts do suggest ways in which we can ritualize the preparatory rite, ways in which we can formulate and express our sentiments. But it should be the actual sentiments of the particular moment of grace, the experience of the living God, that should inspire the rite.

A space of silence, allowing each of us to enter into his own heart, is extremely important at this point in the liturgical celebration. Only in this way can we prepare adequately to enter fully into the prayer of the chosen community and open the inner ear to hear the Good News as Good News spoken to us today. When the president speaks the word of absolution we should know of what we are being absolved and receive the healing and purifying grace deep within our being. Then we will indeed be disposed to rise up to sing with the heavenly choirs and to express the prayer of our hearts to our Father in heaven.

GLORY AND PRAYER

✤ ✤ ✤

The night is chilly—crisp, clear, bright with stars and moonlight. "Silent night, holy night, all is calm, all is bright." The shepherds wrap their fleeces tightly around their lean bodies. Sharp eyes peer out beyond the ring of fire light; ears are alert, sensitive hearts add keenness to their perception—these are good shepherds who love their sheep. They may be ranked rather low in the hierarchy by those who consider themselves judges of the just. But they live out of a native goodness. They sense and respond to the goodness of God in his creation. They care for that creation and are in harmony with it. They care for each other and live in harmony. They are men of good will.

> Glory to God in the highest,
> and peace on earth to those of good will.

The sudden specter dazzles their watching eyes, delights their keen ears. What is this? And what does it mean?

> We know who God's favorites are —
> To the poor he sent angels,
> to the rich, but a star.

If the preparatory rites have achieved their purpose, we are now more truly people of good will. We are more aware of our poverty. The ears of our hearts are more attentive to hear. And the first call we hear may be a summons to ascend before the throne of mercy and, in the company of the angels, to exult in the divine glory.

A fearful yet trusting Jacob laid his weary head on a stone and fell into a deep sleep. Soon he saw a great ladder reaching up to the very throne of God, and on it, angels ascending and descending. The angels came down to lift him, his fears, his hopes, his trust, his humble faithfulness, up to the throne of the Most High. "Truly, God is in this place and I did not know it. How awe inspiring this place is! This is nothing less than the house of God; this is the gate of heaven!"

As a purified people of God gathered together, we constitue a holy place, an indwelling place for God himself. How awesome! We are at the gateway of heaven. We have ready access to the throne of grace. Ministers will bring down to us God's word, his blessing, himself. And we are invited to transcend, to rise up in spirit, to be already with the risen Lord in his heavenly place. As our master promised: "You will see greater things . . . . You will see heaven laid open and, above the Son of Man, the angels of God ascending and descending."

In some of the renewed Eucharistic rites, the *Gloria*, the hymn of the angels, has been placed after Communion. That is perhaps fitting. The angels sang it to the shepherds only after Christ had come down from heaven into the midst of his people. That is a moment *par excellence* for glorifying God, but the fittingness of its being where it is in our rite can be affirmed. We reserve it for feasts and festivals. On such days it seems right that we should, in the spirit of the feast, ascend with the angels to the mystic altar in heaven, there to celebrate in a more transcendent way. On fasts and ferials we might more properly keep our place on earth and humbly raise our petitions to God in heaven. In an earlier tradition, on such days when the president called "Let us pray," all fell to their knees and humbled themselves before God, making petition in their hearts; while on feasts and all during the paschal time the faithful remained standing with the risen Christ, their powerful and present mediator.

Whether we have been lifted up to heavenly places with the angels and have sung his glory or remain solidly on earth, when the president summons us to prayer we can be certain of powerful mediation as we pray through Jesus Christ, the only Son, our Lord, who lives and reigns with the Father and the Holy Spirit. It is important that when we are summoned to prayer we are given time to pray. The president may give direction to our prayers—the missal texts suggest this as an alternate—but he cannot do all the praying for us. His prayer has been traditionally called a collect. He is to collect our prayer, the prayer of the community. So we must have time to pray, to lay before the Lord the concerns that lie in our hearts, so that they may be collected.

We need not in this silent moment scurry to make known to the Lord all our cares and needs. He already knows them. God does hear our prayers— not so much the prayers of our lips, the prayers we articulate, but the real concerns that we hold in our hearts. During this moment of silence we can be before him naked, open, with all our needs, and let surface whatever cry may surface. He knows; he hears.

And the president, too, should be hearing. If he is to collect the prayers of his people he should be listening to their cry to heaven, not with the ears of the flesh, but those of the heart. A sensitive priest seems at this time to be counseled by the Spirit. He has the knack, if that is not too earthy a term, of articulating in his collect what has in fact been flowing from the hearts of the assembled. The missal does give a classical collect as a model. It also offers another example, the rather fullsome prayer written by Father Robert Morehouse, a contemplative monk, who tried to listen to the Church at prayer and to articulate what he was hearing. At times it may be most suitable for the celebrant to use one or other of these model prayers. More often they will need to be spontaneously adapted to the prayer of the moment, or even a quite different prayer may need to be articulated. Whatever it is, it is not the time for the president to give voice to his own personal prayer. In the preceding pause his personal prayer should have been allowed to mingle with the prayers of all the others gathered in the assembly. Now his words should give voice to their common prayer, the prayer of the Church assembled, so that all may indeed express their heartfelt "amen."

We have had our say in penitence, praise, and prayer. Now it is time to sit and listen and give God a chance to have his say.

GOOD NEWS

The liturgy is a school: it effectively teaches us and leads us into reality if we are attentive to what is happening, what is being said.

Have you been aware of what happens at the Gospel of the Mass? The priest or deacon steps up to the lectern and greets the people: "The Lord be with you." And what do we reply? "And also with you." Then he says: "The Holy Gospel according to Saint . . . ." And what do we say? "Glory to you, O Lord!" And what do we say at the end of the Gospel reading? "Praise to you, Lord Jesus Christ." Do you notice what has happened? At first we responded to the priest or deacon: "And also with *you*." Then it is as if he disappears. We say: "Glory to you, *O Lord*! Praise to you, *Lord Jesus Christ*!" The priest, the deacon, is no longer there. As the Constitution on the Liturgy of the Second Vatican Council has stated, when the Gospel is read at the Mass, Jesus Christ again proclaims his Good News. Jesus stand there in person to speak to you and to me. As surely as he spoke to the crowds in Galilee, he speaks now to us.

It is easy for us to sense that this is one of the high points of the Mass. In our culture the summons to stand at attention is a call to be attentive to an especially significant moment. We rise and stand for the proclamation of the Gospel.

But let us go back along the trails of tradition and enter into the fourth-century basilica of San Clemente in the heart of Rome. On the day of a great feast the church is packed. Only a marble enclosure keeps the central area around the altar free. The Pontiff sits on his elevated chair in the center of the eastern apse flanked by the clergy. The choir is working its way through an especially rich and elaborate chant that weaves together texts from various parts of the Scriptures as a reflective commentary on the passage that has just been sung by the subdeacon.

One of the fruits of the recent liturgical renewal has been the reintroduction on Sundays and feasts of two readings before the Gospel reading. Usually one of these is from the Old Testament and the other from the New. In theory these are supposed to prepare us for and lead up to the proclamation of the Good News, the fulfillment of the Old, the source of the New. I must confess I was sometimes hard pressed to see a theme that immediately related all three readings. I was relieved recently when an English scholar who worked on the preparation of the lectionary informed me that, in fact, it was only the first reading, the Old Testament reading, that was chosen in view of the Gospel. The second readings, from Saint Paul or one of the Apostles, were selected independently. The president should be aware of the option to omit one or other of these preparatory readings and should make a responsible judgment as to what will truly be profitable for a particular congregation at a particular liturgy. Quantity does not always equal quality.

The Old Testament reading invites us to enter into the experience of God's people being led gradually into the fullness of the revelation. It sometimes throws oblique light into what we already know, enabling us to perceive the Good News with a new depth and clarity. The intervenient chants, traditionally called graduals or tracts, are to provide space for effective reflection and stimulate it. Today we speak of the responsorial psalm, which is often recited rather than sung, or sung rather quickly. If this is the case it would be well to have a pause before and after the responsory so that personal reflection and assimilation might take place. There is no sense in our being flooded with words that wash quickly over us without an opportunity to penetrate into our consciousness and form our heart.

But let us return to our community gathered in San Clemente. The ministers have arisen. An acolyte goes before the celebrant bearing a golden thurible. Another approaches. They kneel and the Pontiff spreads fragrant incense over the glowing coals and blesses it. The deacon, flanked by torch-bearing acolytes, ascends to the high altar and takes up the richly bejeweled text that has been standing at the center. He bows before the Pontiff, imploring a special blessing for the task at hand. Then the solemn procession makes its way down the sanctuary. The meditative chants have ended. The whole congregation has risen. The cantor leads them in a glad acclamation: "Alleluia! Alleluia! Praise the Lord!" Again and again, with suitable exhortations inserted, they respond:

> Our Savior Jesus Christ has done away with death,
> and brought us to life through his Gospel.

> If anyone loves me, he will hold to my words, and
> my Father will love him, and we will come to him.

The procession approaches the magnificent pulpit and the sacred text is enthroned. All fall to silence. And the deacon opens the dialogue:

The Lord be with you!
    And also with you!

The Holy Gospel according to Saint . . . .
    Glory to you, O Lord!

All stand in awed silence as clouds of fragrant incense ascend, enveloping the sacred text, rising to the exalted mosaic of the glorious Christ enthroned on high, lifting the attention of all, heightening all the senses.

And once again Christ Jesus our Lord proclaims his Good News—the Good News of salvation.

It may not often be possible to surround the proclamation of the Gospel with such fitting and symbolic splendor. But we should try to surround this climactic moment of the Liturgy of the Word with significant dignity. We shouldn't settle for a commonplace binding on the sacred text. If we cannot afford gold or silver, local craft can surely produce a cover of dignity out of fine cloth or other artistic material. The text should never be casually left aside on a credence table or in some other place. It might well have its permanent throne in the sanctuary, or be solemnly carried in at the entrance rite and enthroned upon the altar. The Gospel lectern should be a thing of dignity and beauty. We shouldn't forget that just as our God is truly present in his Eucharist in the tabernacle, he is truly present in his Word on the lectern. Although the early Church lavished much more attention on the Gospel pulpit, we, with our developed awareness of the real presence in the Eucharist, should lavish equal attention on both tabernacle and Gospel throne.

Whenever there is a community present it should be easy enough to call forth two acolytes to surround the proclamation with the splendor of lighted tapers. It is the Light of Life that the deacon is setting forth for our illumination. And people today, especially the young, respond to incense as an experience of the fragrance of Christ.

How good is the Good News, and all that surrounds it should be good—the best!

RESPONSE

❊ ❊ ❊

We live in an age of communication. A man steps on the moon and within seconds millions of people on earth both hear and see him. A spacecraft hurtling past the distant planets sends back to us colored pictures of exotic scenery. A flood in Bengal, a skirmish in Las Malvinas, a crop failure in Utrusk is soon witnessed in homes around the world, thanks to satellites that constantly circle our globe. The most remote and primitive village has its prized transistor radio. Judging from the effort and means expended in beaming broadcasts, there is a firm conviction that there are countless electronic and human ears listening from behind the iron and bamboo curtains.

Representatives of all nations regularly gather in assemblies of all sorts. We believe communication is the way to peace. And this is true of the most intimate level as well as on the international level. The key to marital peace in the program of "Marriage Encounter" is "ten and ten"—each day the spouses write to each other for ten minutes and talk frankly to each other for ten minutes. All friendship is based on communication— communication of all sorts. In racial tensions, tensions between management and labor, and all other conflicts we can hope for peaceful and productive resolution through communication, for in the end we are all in this together, we all seek ultimately the same thing, whether we know it or not: we seek the happiness God intends for us. Communication supports us in realizing and being true to our quest. Recovering alcoholics gather daily or even several times in the day just to communicate, and in that communication they support one another in the struggle for life. This is the genius of Alcoholics Anonymous.

The age of communication is, then, a good age, an age very consonant with the deepest aspirations of the human person, with the plan of God. God made us to be happy with him, communicating in his happiness and love. When he was spurned, he did not cease to reach out. He spoke to us first and repeatedly through his prophets and ultimately through his Son. He himself descended Jacob's ladder and became one with us. He taught us the way, the truth, and the meaning of life. And before finally ascending the ladder he charged chosen ones to go forth and teach all nations. Communication is a key in the mission of his Church. When that Church gathered in the Second Vatican Council, its first published document was on communication.

Communication calls for response, even if it is only the response of active listening. Without some response there is no communication—only sounds and images going out into space. All communication, then, is dialogical.

Have you ever noticed that the Mass is dialogical? When we gather, we are responding to a call—the dialogue has already begun. Coming into the presence of a God so good, so completely and constantly a gift, we can only be very conscious of our own rather habitual lack of response, and we sense a need to express our repentance and conversion. God responds through the priestly word of absolution. Then we praise him and ask for his continual help. He responds with his life-giving words. To this we respond in a variety of ways: reflective silence and song, profession of faith, confident petition, and gifts that symbolize the gift of ourselves. God accepts our gifts and changes them into his very self and gives us himself in that consummation of communication we call Communion. We again respond with reflective silence and song, and confident prayer that our whole life might be a response to his love. He responds with his blessing and the charge to go forth and share in communicating all that we have received.

God's verbal communication to us in the Mass reaches its height in the proclamation of the Gospel, the Good News.

I often say that Mother Church is a good Jewish Mother. This is so in many ways. I experience it at Mass in the way she feeds me. When I join a Jewish family for a meal, Mama usually piles my plate so high with food that if I ate it all I would surely have indigestion and end up enjoying none of it. I have to pick and choose. So, too, at the liturgy, especially on Sundays and feasts with three readings, Mother Church gives me so much that if I try to retain it all I will lose it. Often I have had the experience of being attentive at Mass, but later, when someone asked me about the day's readings, I was completely blank. I could remember nothing. Have you experienced the same? What did the Lord say to you the last time you were at Mass?

At the end of the readings we need to stop for a moment to pick and choose. At our community liturgy we always have a pause at the end of the readings. From out of the flood of words that have poured over us we need to pick a word—a phrase, a thought, an idea—to carry with us. In the silence after Communion we might reflect upon this word with the

Lord and then carry it with us as we go forth into the day's or evening's activities. I find that in the course of the day this word will often come alive, it will respond in a special way to a particular person or happening. I feel that if each day I can truly assimilate one word of the Lord, I will come to have the mind of Christ.

If there is no homily—and there doesn't need to be one—we can sit in silence and let the Spirit, whom the Father and Jesus sent to teach us all things, do the homilizing. But if there is a homily, I think its main function should be to help us choose a life-giving word. It might serve as a sort of underscore. The president, in the grace of his office, can assist us in hearing a word of life clearly and effectively. The homily should not bring in anything extraneous. It should not interrupt the form of the dialogue of the Mass, the dialogue going on between the people assembled and the God who assembled them. The homily should flow from the word that has been proclaimed, or place it in context, giving it an enhancing frame. The homily is not the occasion to introduce extraneous affairs. Announcements can be put in a bulletin or be part of the sending forth at the end of the Mass, part of the way one effectively takes the fruit of the Mass back into life. The homily is the time to hear the Lord and prepare to respond.

The Good News is essentially a person. God tells us about himself, even about his inmost secrets ("I call you friends because I make known to you all that the Father has made known to me"), but he also does far more: for us and for our salvation he personally came down from heaven. Our response, then, is first of all to a person, to who he is, to what he says because of who he is. This is faith, and in response to his proclamation we proclaim our faith:

> We believe in one God . . . .
> We believe in one Lord, Jesus Christ . . . .
> We believe in the Holy Spirit, the Lord . . . .

This is a very personal moment; we put ourselves on the line. Or at least that is what our response should mean. We commit ourselves to convictions that should shape every aspect of our lives. Unfortunately, there is faith and there is faith. To use Cardinal Newman's happy phrasing, our rational assent needs to become a real assent. We assent—I almost wrote "easily enough"—we assent to the notions, the ideas, the propositions of faith. But that is not really the whole picture. To be able to say yes even to the notions of faith is a gift from the Lord. And it requires on our part a certain humility—that humility which is truth, which truthfully acknowledges that God does know more than we can figure out and that it is wise to listen to him.

But assenting to the truths of faith is relatively easy compared to living according to them faithfully. This is the response God wants; and a real assent, a deep conviction welling up within us that says "Yes, yes, that is it, that is the reality" greatly supports us in giving such a response. This is one of the reasons why, again and again, we rise in our assembly and proclaim our faith in this way. Through constant repetition the creed can move from our even inattentive words down into our hearts and change our notional assent into an ever more real assent, an effective assent.

As we recite the creed within the gathered community, it is a very personal moment. It renews that moment when, in person or through sponsors, we first took the step to become a part of the people. It is also a historical moment. While we affirm our intention to live and die at one with the community of faith, we use a formula that arose out of the blood of many martyrs, the struggles of many confessors of the faith, the reflections of many Fathers of the Church, and that has expressed the faith of millions through sixteen centuries and more. In articulating our faith in this creed we enter into a great current that will continue to flow until the end of time.

It is also a cosmic moment. One of the memories of my student days in Rome never fails to stir my imagination. Seventy thousand of us are standing in the immense cavern of Saint Peter's Basilica. We are all colors—red, yellow, black, white, tan, brown. We are from many more nations than one can readily name. We babble in many languages. Then—and it always seemed suddenly—the Vicar of Christ is in our midst, and the whole vast throng, as if with one voice, sings out mightily, so that the gilded vaults high above us seem to roll with echoes:

> Credo in unum Deum . . . .
> Credo in unum Dominum Jesum Christum . . . .
> Credo in Spiritum Sanctum Dominum . . . .

The Church Universal, gathered around its one Supreme Pastor, proclaims its one faith. Every creed ever said, even in the smallest of congregations in the most remote of mission chapels, in jungle huts or in Siberian prison camps, on battleships or on the summit of Tabor, is one with this creed being proclaimed at the heart of Christendom—and with the creed we proclaim today in our parish church or monastic choir. It is the expression of the mind and heart of the one body of Christ: We believe!

And because of that belief, of all that we profess in that creed, we can confidently pray. The creed makes us aware of our dependence: he is the Maker, we are the made; he is the Savior, we are the saved. It makes us aware, too, of how much we are loved: "for us and for our salvation . . . ."

It makes us aware of what has been promised us, and so we can confidently pray.

The priest may start us off, perhaps giving an additional stir to our faith and confidence. Then he or another will start the flow of petitions. All our prayer is response. For it is God who has given us a basis for asking, the sensitivity to our needs, and the love that inspires us to care for the needs of others. We pray for the Church—his body and ours; we pray for civil society, of which we are also members; we pray for all those concerns that press on our individual and corporate hearts.

We pray because he told us to pray. We pray because he answers prayers. We pray now to give direction to our offering. We confidently lay all our petitions at his feet, knowing they will be there before him and will be cared for as we enter into the great prayer.

BREAKING THE BREAD OF THE WORD

✤ ✤ ✤

Evening gatherings were common enough in those days, even though the brothers and sisters were often quite weary after a long day's labor. But one night was special for it would be the last chance they would have to hear Paul before he set out for Assos and on toward Jerusalem. The upper room was crowded and overheated with the press of bodies. The smoky oil lamps added to the oppressive air.

Eutychus had found what was probably the best possible location for his weary body, or so it seemed. Perched on the windowsill he did not have to stand on his aching feet. At the same time he got the benefit of any breeze that stirred in the night. Paul was a fascinating preacher. A passion burned in him, a passion for Jesus Christ—he knew in whom he believed— and a passion for them, his hearers, his beloved children begotten of God in the Gospel. His imagery was very lively and sometimes very earthy; he called a spade a spade. But sometimes his theology could get quite intricate —even the Apostle Peter admitted to difficulties in understanding him— and he did tend to go on and on, piling one powerful insight on top of another. It was too much, especially on this last night when he seemed to be trying to say it all.

It was too much for Eutychus. His mind began to wander, then his heavy eyelids began to close. He lost his precarious balance. Suddenly there was a shriek and a terrible corporate gasp as Eutychus disappeared out the window. It was three full stories to the street below. Some rushed to the door, others to the windows. Paul with quiet dignity and purpose followed those who clambered down the narrow stairway. As he emerged from the door the crowd that had gathered around the inert figure opened to allow him to approach. If a compassionate fatherly heart ever revealed itself in a face it was now as Paul looked down upon the young man. His eyes glistened with tears that had not yet begun to flow. He had wanted his words to give this boy life and now he was confronted with death. But Paul's heart was too much out there to turn in with self-recrimination. Rather his love called forth his faith, as Peter's had done, as his Master's had done. He resolutely reached down and took Eutychus's hand and helped him to rise—literally, to rise from the dead.

Fortunately most homilies are not preached in an upper room with listeners balancing on windowsills, for most homilies do not seem to have the kind of faith that raises the dead. Usually they share Paul's other ability —that of putting listeners to sleep.

The homily is the climactic moment of what used to be called the Mass of the Catechumens but is today called, more happily, the Liturgy of the Word. It is a moment of communion when the leader of the assembly breaks the bread of the Word and shares this source of life: living faith— *the just person lives by faith.*

After due preparation the community is given the gift of the Word. Indeed, there has already been a certain sharing of faith in their very coming together, especially on the part of the readers in the way they have proclaimed the Word and on the part of the singers in the way they have led the responsive meditation on it. But now all turn to the one they look upon as their leader in this community celebration, the one who in a special way represents Christ in their midst ("presiding in the person of Christ," says the General Instruction in the missal) and they wait for him to share his faith, to enlighten their minds, and to feed their hungry souls.

The community is not looking for the homilist to advertise the "book learning" he got in the seminary or in his ongoing studies, though they hope that such study solidly grounds his faith-filled insight. They are not looking for amusing anecdotes or interesting stories, though they do want him to relate what he says to their personal lives and they appreciate it when he does this with a certain humor. (The sublimity of life is often shot through with humor. Even boys falling out of windows during sermons has its humor, especially when the preacher raises them up—and goes right on preaching!)

Mother Church is a good Jewish mother. When it comes to feeding her children she heaps the portions one atop the other. Not just one good rich reading, or two. The Sunday and feast-day menu calls for three generous portions. If we try to digest it all we will no doubt suffer from indigestion and profit not at all. What we look to our homilist to do is to choose some particularly nourishing morsel or two—three at the very most—and serve it up to us in such a way that we can get the very most out of it. He will have savored the meal through the week and thoroughly digested it so that he will be able to highlight each morsel's very special flavor and give us the compacted Word that will energize our coming week if not our entire life.

We want life, and to have it more abundantly; and we want proof in the liveliness of the homilist that what he feeds to us is life giving. Our Master said, *You judge a tree by its fruit.* Is the Word producing the fruits of the Spirit in our preacher: love, joy, peace, kindliness? If this is evident, we will eagerly listen. We are all looking for the answers, at least those answers that can make living the questions of life worthwhile. We know our Master has all the answers. But how are we to get them? *They will never hear unless they get a preacher.* What we want to see in our homilist is a man who has heard and gotten out of the Word that we have just heard together a Word of life, an answer to some of life's questions, or at least an insight that makes living with the questions good—a realization that the Way, no matter how obscure he may seem to be, is the Truth that is Life. Does the homilist know in whom he believes and is he willing to share with us now how he has heard and experienced him in today's readings? When the priest finishes proclaiming the Gospel he kisses the text. It is a very intimate moment. He and his Master touch lips, share breath. He wants to be enlivened and his lips to be purified so that he may without any impediment speak the life-giving Word of Life.

A homily is not a lecture. Nor is it primarily a work of exegesis, though it may be fundamentally that. The homily is not the time to interrupt the flow of the communal experience of a specific encounter with the Christ to introduce some extraneous concern, no matter how important. Though, in fact, no concern is extraneous to the Christ and if the homilist has allowed the given text to penetrate deeply into his being it will enliven and illuminate any concern he feels called to share with his people. But the concern has to be deeply rooted in the received Word and not superficially attached or it will not only interrupt the present experience of the community but court rejection because of its jarring intrusion.

In proclaiming the Gospel, the priest is not just telling the two-thousand-year-old story of the historical Jesus. He is sharing the story of Christ, yesterday, today, and the same forever—the story of the whole Christ, his own story, the story of the community gathered. We want to hear his lived experience of the story. We want to hear how he is experiencing the story lived out in us, all of us together in the community of the Christ-living-today. He helps us get in touch with the story as it is unfolding in our lives. He wipes some of the film from our eyes of faith so that we see something more of the enthralling wonder of salvation history coming to its consummation in us. The homilist is not exegeting a text, he is sharing an event in which we are all participating.

Appeals for money are problematic. They do need to be made *at times*. The Word does call us forth to generosity and compassion. The regular collection should be rightly integrated into the offering of the Mass. But in most instances particular calls for special needs among God's people can be better left to that part of the Mass where we are being summoned to mission, to reach out of our fullness to share what we have received.

The homily should at times evoke our care and effective concern; this is part of Christian life, but that life itself needs to be fed and strengthened so that it can be responsive. When Christian life is well fed it will respond without being asked or prodded.

Our first response to the Word should be "Yes, that's it! I believe." It is good to have a pause after the homily so we can reflectively absorb the point the celebrant has made and be in touch with the experience, so that the Word of life he has underlined can come to life in us. Then we rise up and say our yes in the words of a profession of faith that goes back to the fourth century. We join hands as part of a living tradition and, empowered by such solidarity, we proclaim: "We believe in one God, the Father, the Almighty . . . in one Lord, Jesus Christ, the only Son of God . . . in the Holy Spirit, the Lord, the giver of life," and in all that they are, have done, and have revealed. As we together reaffirm our full acceptance and commitment to this faith-known reality, which is the context of our lives, we affirm in particular our acceptance and adhesion to the Word of life spoken to us at this Mass. We commit ourselves to living it. If the homilist has failed to give us a word that calls us forth we have then to take our own word from the Gospel or one of the other readings. But we need to take a concrete word of life so we can go forth from this community celebration with a basis for growth and fuller life.

We need help, of course. Of ourselves we can do nothing. Only by God's goodness and generosity do we exist, are we able to receive faith and life as just ones and live by that faith. The Prayer of the Faithful should be first and foremost a prayer *for* the faithful. Our Lord said the second great commandment, like unto the first, is to love our neighbor as we love ourselves. Therefore we must first love ourselves. Psychologists will confirm this. It is a law written into the fabric of our nature. And experience certainly confirms it. When we are in touch with our own magnificence, then we can truly blossom in all our beauty and we can rejoice in and foster the full flowering and beauty of everyone else. When we are not in touch with our own beauty, our own magnificence, not living out of our own fullness, we can hardly tolerate that others do. We become defensive and competitive. Rather than truly wanting others to increase, we tend to want to put them down so that we can look better by comparison. Let us first pray for our own fullness in grace and life so that we can pray from the heart, pray for the same for others.

When we are deeply in touch with ourselves we know that we are part of a whole. Our humanity is part of the whole fabric of the created human family, and baptism has given us an even deeper and more significant oneness with others in Christ. So in praying for ourselves in the Prayer of the Faithful we pray first for the whole Christ, our head on earth and all our members; we pray for the Church. Then we pray for the society, the structures and leadership of humanity. And then we touch on the particular needs that press upon our hearts. It is an expansive moment.

If we listen to our own prayers and the prayers of our assembly they are very telling. They tell us how catholic we are, where our concerns and sensitivity lie. If the leader of the liturgy calls us to this prayer in a perfunctory way, just reading some formula from a book, the prayer that follows is very apt to be rather perfunctory and by rote. The formulas in the sacramentary are meant simply to be models or guides for formulation. The call to prayer should arise out of the experience of God the community has just shared in his Word. It should convey a faith conviction that will call us forth to pray now with faith and conviction. The one who leads the prayer, if there be one formulating the petitions, should also be coming from the present experience of the community. Some leaders may well sense a need to have some prepared petitions. These should be prepared in the context of a prayerful listening to the day's readings. yet there should still be an opening of heart that will not preclude a reformulation of the petitions at the time of their statement according to the movement of the Spirit and the experience of the Word in the preceding readings and homily. It certainly is good if some time and space is allowed for petitions to arise from the immediate faith experience of the members of the community, although this presents practical difficulties in large congregations. A period of silence for personal interior formulations culminating in a general petition by the leader is a step in the right direction. But above all, this prayer is the prayer of the faithful, and every effort should be made to allow it to arise from among the faithful gathered.

When Nicodemus, a wise leader of the Jewish people, sought from the Lord a deeper understanding of the inner workings of Christ's redemptive grace, Jesus responded with an image: *The wind blows wherever it pleases; you hear its sound, but you cannot tell where it comes from or where it is going.* And that is how it is with those who are being moved and brought to fullness by the Spirit: *That is how it is with all who are born of the Spirit.* Christ's late-born apostle, Paul, said, *We do not know how to pray as we ought, but the Holy Spirit prays within us.* In our prayer we should not try to dictate to God how he should act. Like Mary, we lay our concerns confidently before the Lord and leave it to him to respond to them in the way he knows is best. And his response will be beyond our expectations: *They have no wine. . . . You have kept the best wine till last.* God always hears our prayer, but often he does not respond the way we might expect or want. He looks to our deepest hearts, sees the deep longings from which our present petitions arise, and he responds in the way that will best fulfill those deep longings.

The Profession of Faith and the Prayer of the Faithful are a transition space in the liturgy. The Liturgy of the Word reaches its consummation in the proclamation of the Gospel and its homiletic assimilation. The Litury of the Eucharist begins with bringing our gifts to the altar. The Profession of Faith and the Prayer of the Faithful are a response to the former and a preparation for the latter. The creed is often omitted. It would be unfortunate if the prayer was also omitted and there was no completing response and transition space. If the circumstances allow for nothing more, it would be good for the homilist to complete his word with a reflective pause and then a prayerful response—a few petitions, space for petitions from the community, and a collect. We are then ready to carry the fullness of the experience of God and of ourselves, of the whole Christ and of the whole of humanity, which we have entered into in the Liturgy of the Word, to the altar to be transubstantiated in the liturgy of covenant and thanksgiving—the Eucharist.

BLESSED ART THOU

✤ ✤ ✤

Blessed art Thou, O Lord our God, King of the universe, who created the fruit of the vine.

Blessed art Thou, O Lord our God, who hast chosen us for Thy service from among the nations, exalting us by making us holy through Thy commandments. In love hast Thou given us, O Lord our God, holidays for joy and festivals for gladness. Thou didst give us this Feast of Unleavened Bread, the season of our freedom, in commemoration of our liberation from Egypt. Thou hast chosen us for Thy service from among the nations and hast sanctified us by giving us, with love and gladness, Thy holy festivals as a heritage. Blessed art Thou, O Lord, who hallowest Israel and the Festivals.

Blessed art Thou, O Lord our God, King of the universe, who hast kept us in life, who hast preserved us, who hast enabled us to reach this season.

Thus the venerable patriarch of the family gathered around the festive table inaugurated the ancient rite of the Haggadah, the Seder meal. The *Kiddush* is complete, and all drink wine.

Then two children bring a pitcher of water, a bowl, and a towel. Each one washes his hands, the ceremony of *Urchatz*, symbolizing the purification necessary to enter into this religious service.

Soon the father takes up the matzah, the unleavened bread that represents the people: "Lo! This is the bread. . . ."

Any Christian privileged to sit at the table or witness this family liturgy quickly senses a continuity between this ancient rite and the offering of the gifts at Mass. In the recent renewal of the Eucharistic liturgy, the elaborate offertory rite that had developed over the course of the Middle Ages was set aside and the Mass was brought back to its simpler origins.

It was at a family liturgy, a Seder meal prepared by Peter and John, that Jesus gathered his special friends, his chosen twelve, and celebrated the first Mass. He went through the elaborate and richly beautiful rite.

He himself took the role of the children and sevants, and washed not their hands, but their feet. They listened together to the readings, or more properly, the recitation of the sacred texts appropriate to the feast. The psalms of the Hallel were sung. Thanksgiving was given. Finally, as the ritual meal neared completion, the *Afikoman*, the last piece of matzah, was taken up, and a new rite was inaugurated. "Take, eat, this is my body, which is given for you." And with the final cup of wine: "Take this, all of you, and drink from it: This is the cup of my blood, the blood of the new and everlasting covenant. It will be shed for you and for all so that sins may be forgiven."

If the renewed offertory rite is much simpler, it is also much richer— pregnant with symbolism and association. It takes us back to the first Mass, the Last Supper, and to our Jewish origins, to the divine liberation from bondage, to salvation history. If you have never had the privilege of sharing in a Seder meal it would be well to seek the opportunity. Or perhaps celebrate a similar meal with fellow Christians. Texts with detailed instructions and explanations are readily available. Parish groups might consider sponsoring a Seder meal early in Holy Week in preparation for Holy Thursday and the Christian community's renewal of the Last Supper.

Our simple offertory rite does not only reach back through history. It reaches down deep into human reality. What is offered is food and drink, bread and wine—essential staples of the Lord's people. They are what sustains life; they are the fruit of life's labors collaborating with the divine munificence active in our creation. *Blessed are you, Lord, God of all creation. Through your goodness we have this bread to offer, which earth has given and human hands have made. . . . Through your goodness we have this wine to offer, fruit of the vine and work of human hands.* Our labor, our sustenance, our life, we bring to the altar. It is an integral offering.

At certain periods in our history the faithful brought to their weekly celebration of the Eucharist whatever was indeed the fruit of their labor: vegetables, eggs, milk, cheese, woven cloth, shoes, candles, a bench— whatever was the "work of human hands." While most of this was set aside to sustain the life of God's minister—the Old Testament clearly prescribed what portions went to the priests and servers—and to relieve the needs of the poor, the priest selected bread and wine, consecrating them with the opening words of the *Kiddush*, before he washed his hands and proceeded with the *memoria*: "Do this in memory of me."

He chose bread and wine not only because his Master had done so, not only because they were the most basic staples, but also because of their rich intrinsic symbolism. One of the earliest patristic texts concerning the Eucharist contains these words:

> As the grains of wheat spread out on the mountainside have been
> gathered into unity in this bread, so gather your Church into unity.

Bread is very rich in symbolism. First of all, a grain of wheat has to fall
into the ground and die so that there can be many grains. The death of
Christ is the source of all Christians' lives. The grains are mowed down,
dried, threshed, sacked, milled, bleached, mixed, and baked to become a
bread that can be transformed into Christ and nourish. The whole of their
surface identity, their individuality, is obliterated—only then can each
grain make its essential contribution and be a part of the whole, transformed into a life-giving sacrament of the glorified Christ.

And so, too, the grapes become wine.

In many churches today communicants place their own host or bit of
bread on the plate. In other churches, at the offertory, a representative
group carries bread and wine to the priest. In either case, this is an important reflective moment. We are invited to step into the stream of a very
ancient and rich tradition, and to step out of the depths of our own in-
dividualism. That bit of unleavened bread reminds us that a people were
freed by God in a rush of dramatic life. There was no time to leaven the
dough and let it rise. In the rush of our active lives, if we bring what we
have, who we are, to the Lord, he will lead us into freedom. He will make
a covenant with us, an everlasting covenant of love.

Wine, too, is well chosen. As the Psalmist reminds us, God made wine
to rejoice our hearts. The Eucharistic meal is to be a joyful meal, a
thanksgiving, in which we are conscious of our many blessings. *Blessed
are you, Lord God, because you have . . . .* It is certainly desirable that all
those who share in the Eucharist should not only participate in the offering of the wine, but should have the joy of having their inners warmed by
communicating in it.

It is quite common now for a collection to be taken up at this time of
the offertory. Unfortunately, in Catholic churches, this is done as the
priest goes on with the rite at the altar, and perhaps, too, with the congregation singing a song. One gets the feeling that we are a bit ashamed
of introducing this money-gathering into the rite; we would rather not
see it as part of the rite. It is just something that happens incidentally,
concomitantly. After all, isn't money "the root of all evil"?

Such an attitude would be unfortunate. In times past, the faithful
brought the fruit of the labor of their hands to the offertory as a symbol of
themselves. And so should we today. The fruit of our labor today usually
takes the form of money. When we bring to the offertory plate our dollar
bills we are bringing our labor and sweat, our creativity and fatigue, all
portions of our very lives. The collection should be a significant and
reflective action, a real part of the offertory rite, a personal entering into

and participating in the offering of Christ, our Head. Far better is the way the collection more commonly takes place in Protestant churches: while the plate is passed, all sit quietly; perhaps the organ plays gently in the background. There is an invitation to reflect on what we are doing. When all have made their offering, the plates are carried solemnly to the foot of the altar or Communion table, where the pastor receives them. He then turns and raises them up to God. He may even place them on the altar in a specially wrought offertory plate. The symbolism is complete.

Before concluding our reflection on the offertory of the Mass, I would like to note a practice that is growing in many Christian communities. It harkens back in its own way to the early custom of bringing various offerings—whatever was the fruit of one's labor—to the Eucharistic offering. Today, parishioners are being urged to bring to Mass foodstuffs, various staples, and even clothes, which can be made available to the poor of the parish. It is well if these offerings are seen as part of the rite of bringing the gift of oneself to Christ. This invites us to be more aware of the whole Christ. "Whatever you do to the least of my brethren you do to me." In giving to the brethern, to the poor, we give to Christ. And, too, it reminds us that Christ himself is all gift; whatever he received he gave to others, and so he continues. And we, who by baptism are one with Christ, other-Christs, are—if we are to be true to ourselves—to do likewise.

Unfortunately the offertory rite of the Mass can be a hurried thing, done with little time for reflection and virtually no community participation. It can be done as almost a private business of the priest, carried out while the congregation is occupied with a hymn. A well-chosen hymn can have its place, but it should not obscure the symbolic rite that is taking place. Reflective music might set a better context, enabling us to focus our attention on the offering as it is brought through the hands of the priest into the offering of Christ.

The ritual allows for the use of incense in this rite. And this is excellent. Its sweet odor, the sight of the clouds of fragrant smoke ascending, invite a more integral association with the goodness of our giving to the Lord. More wholeheartedly can we then respond to the priest's bidding: "Pray, brethren, that our sacrifice may be acceptable to God, the almighty Father."

> May the Lord accept the sacrifice at your hands, for the praise and glory of his name, for our good, and the good of all his Church, and the whole human family.

The celebrant again collects all the movement, all the aspiration, all the hopes, and all the prayer of the assembled community, and brings the offertory rite to completion in such way that all can express a heartfelt amen.

IN HEAVENLY PLACES:
HOLY, HOLY, HOLY

❊   ❊   ❊

Holy, holy, holy, Lord God of Hosts . . . . The prophet shook in his sandals. For his eyes beheld the unseeable, the very glory of God. The Temple —Jerusalem's great wonder, Solomon's glory, he recognized it immediately —stood before him in prophetic vision. It was filled with light and splendor. All around it flew the great glistening six-winged seraphs. They moved, but they did not. While two great wings held them aloft, two others were folded before them concealing their lower part, and with the last two they covered their faces as they worshiped the great Glory. Isaiah had no wings to veil his face. He could only stand naked before the Splendor that filled all the courts of the Temple. There, high above the holy place, he sat enthroned: the Lord God of Hosts, "Woe is me! For I am lost; for I am a man of unclean lips, and I dwell in the midst of a people of unclean lips; for my eyes have seen the King, the Lord of Hosts!" The seraphim cried out unceasingly: "Holy, holy, holy is the Lord of Hosts; the whole earth is full of your glory." And this man of unclean lips could not join in.

But we dare to join with all the heavenly hosts and sing: *Holy, holy, holy . . . for blessed is he who comes*—our Lord, our Savior, our Redeemer. Thanks to him, not only our lips, but our whole being, has been cleansed.

Our gifts have been brought to the altar. The president has asked us to pray that his sacrifice and ours will be acceptable to God our Father. And we have so prayed. The offertory rite is complete and we are ready for the great prayer that transcends all time and place and makes present the greatest act of all creation as it abides forever in the "eternal now" of God. We are indeed to go up into heavenly places and be one with the eternal choirs, who with us glorify God, in and through Christ our Lord. Before we enter in, so that we might enter in as we ought, some preparation is in order. We need to recall for a moment our way thereto.

The Lord be with you—for without him we can do nothing, least of all stand worthily before the Lord of Hosts.

Lift up you hearts. Yes, for we are to ascend to the very summits of creation, and enter into communion with the heavenly hosts, and know that the time of our salvation is here.

Let us give thanks to the Lord, our God. This is Eucharist, the great prayer of thanksgiving. We do as he told us. We do this in memory of him, in gratitude for all that he has done for us, he who loved us till the end.

It is right that we should always and everywhere give him thanks and praise. There is so much for which to thank and praise God that we can never cease, we can never sum it up—the magnificent revelation of his goodness in the creation and, ultimately, in the mysteries of Christ and his Church. The preface to the fourth Eucharistic Prayer and the Anaphora of Saint Basil from which it is derived try to expresss such a summation. But the preface ordinarily brings to our attention one particular facet of God's loving economy, the one of the season, or of the feast, or of this particular celebration.

In the earliest days it was for the presiding bishop or priest to formulate this praise and thanksgiving. He knew what at that moment made God's loving action particularly present to the community and he evoked it. At the paschal season it may have been the community's consciousness of the presence of the risen Lord in their midst. At Christmas they might be filled with the expectation of the renewing graces of the Incarnation. Or the occasion might be the celebration of a local saint who, in his relics, was present in their midst; it might be the incorporation of a new sister through baptism, or a marriage, or the death of one of their own. The president would sing out of a full heart:

> Father, all-powerful and ever-living God, we do well always
> and everywhere to give you thanks through Jesus Christ our
> Lord. Today...
> This day...
> Now...
> Every year...

The Eucharistic Prayer, too, was at first left very much to the president of the assembly. Gradually, standard forms began to emerge. As the Roman Canon began to be normative, so too did the prefaces that went with it. The prayer always retained a few variables for the great feasts. And its preface also retained a small selection of texts for feasts and seasons. Special interests over the centuries occasionally added others: for the Sacred Heart, for the Holy Eucharist, for Christ the King, for Saint Joseph. With the dawning of liturgical renewal, a gradual enrichment began with the addition of the prefaces for the Advent season. And things have moved on from there. Many of the new Eucharistic Prayers have their own prefaces, though in most cases the priest is free to choose another. We now have over forty seasonal prefaces, fourteen different ones for the feasts of Christ, sixteen for Mary and the saints—not counting the many approved for particular groups; we Cistercians have special prefaces for Saint Benedict and Saint Bernard—and others for special celebrations: marriages, ordinations, religious professions, funerals, and special holidays like Independence Day and Thanksgiving Day. Within some of these formulas there is room for adaptations to the more particular.

All of this places a new responsibility on the presiding priest. He must prepare for the particular celebration and carefully choose the most fitting text. Then, within the celebration, he will have to be sensitive and capture the movement of the particular assembly so that he can most effectively call them forth from their present experience to the fullest participation in the great prayer, to the liveliest sense of oneness with the celebrations of heaven. It is here where the eternal fullness of redemptive love is brought into the here and now of a particular Christian community and made relevant. The president wants to put his finger on just what this particular group celebrating here and now senses as the most moving reason why they should do Eucharist, and give voice to that in such a way that all can identify with it and be drawn more fully into the great prayer. If the formulas available seem to fail him and he cannot bring one of them to express what he knows should be said, then he can take the opportunity to speak more directly and spontaneously to the assembly. This is one of the places where the General Instruction in the Missal specifically says this can be done. It was perhaps because not all priests could formulate expressive yet concise texts that certain formulas became normative. Even today, although liturgical studies and training have come a long way, many priests do not feel prepared to adapt the texts to the particular celebration. They will find it easier, and it can still be very effective, to say a few words of their own before taking up one of the formulated texts.

Some liturgists object to the name "preface." They note, and rightly, that this address to the Father is fully part of the Eucharistic Prayer. But it does serve, with its hortatory dialogue and its articulated motivation, to call us forth. It invites us to rise with and through our particular immediate concern to the fuller context of the great prayer, to the vast context of salvation history, to the culminating and all-pervasive act of eternal love. It invites us to transcend our particular gathering, or rather, bring our gathering into the great communion of all worshipers of all times, of all the saints and angels. It invites us in the great prayer of Christ to his Father to come into heavenly places. *Lift up your hearts . . . and sing: Holy, holy, holy.*

IN MEMORY OF ME

✤ ✤ ✤

The meal had been moving along at its majestic ritual pace. The first cups of wine had been drunk after the blessing of the *Kiddush*. There was that startling moment at the *Urchatz* when a servant should have come forward to wash their hands. As usual—it had happened so many times before—the twelve were jockeying for places at table, arguing who was to take precedence. John's special place none could deny—all shared the Lord's special love for the youngest among them. But his precedence among them was not one of authority—Peter in his forcefulness seemed to assume that role. Whether the Lord endorsed his assumption was another question. He had said to Peter: "You are Peter, and on this rock [*petra*] I will build my Church." But he also reprimanded Peter's presumptuousness and even called him Satan.

As companions for special moments, the Lord chose James, John, and Peter. James, using John's nearness to the Lord as well as his mother's charm and loving service, tried to get recognition for himself, but the Master gently put him off. Now, as they chided each other, they forgot Jesus' parable about the marriage feast, with its concluding words: "The first shall be last and the last first." No one seemed to be pushing for the last place. Then suddenly Jesus was standing there, girding himself with a towel and washing not their hands, but their feet! In their embarrassing humiliation only Peter had the brashness to speak out, and he was quickly turned around. Yes, their Lord and Master taught them an unforgettable lesson this time. The *Urchatz* should always remind them of it.

Then things moved along in order: they had eaten *Karpas*, some celery or parsley, and the matzah was broken (*Yachatz*) and raised up (*Maggeed*), reminding them of their afflictions, the afflictions of their people, so they could hear again with thanksgiving the tale of their deliverance. John had asked the traditional questions and the Master had answered. But there was something special about his answers. There were new implications. They drank the second cup more thoughtfully. *Dayaynou*, "it is enough for us." But is it enough? The Master promises more. As they chanted the Hallel Psalms and again shared the cup, the sense of the specialness of this night increased. Judas had gone out on a mysterious mission. The Master spoke of betrayal. There was talk of swords and cockcrow. And now he said he would not drink of the cup again until they drank it in the kingdom. What was going to happen this night?

Then the Master took the *Afikoman*, the piece of matzah that he had set aside, broke it into pieces for each, and said: "Take, eat, this is my body, which will be broken for you." He filled his cup, said the final thanksgiving, and held out the cup to them. "Take this and drink from it, all of you. This is the cup of my blood, the blood of the new covenant, which will be shed for you." Here was something new—very new, fulfilling the old. All the mysterious allusions of the evening, and so much more, came together. This powerful moment of communion and enlightenment would fade in the weariness, fear, confusion, and seemingly ultimate disaster of that night. But afterward they would remember well his words: "Do this in memory of me."

Make this *memoria*—"memory" does not adequately translate the word. "Memory" here is not just a calling to mind, not just making the event present in imagination or by symbolic representation. It is more. It is making the very reality present now as then. How can this be?

To answer this question we have to step into another realm, the realm of faith, where we can begin to see things as God sees them. As we see things naturally in the course of time, one event follows another and then passes into history. Not so with God. He lives, he is, an "eternal now." All that ever was and ever will be is present and actual in him now. It never ceases to have its full actuality. It is not past. It is not future. It is.

Let me try to express this graphically. We see things, as it were, extended in a long line, moving along, coming up to the present and then moving away into the past. The events of history are stretched out over the long procession of history. For God, though, they are, as it were, all piled up in one single spot, all together in the moment we call "now." They are all here, now, for him. By our faith we can reach out of our time into his eternal now and touch any thing as truly existing now in him.

In God's eternal now the whole created reality is now present. If we picture it as all piled up, at the summit, closest to God, most like him, the ultimate act of all creation is the greatest act of love in that creation. It is the closest to God, the most like him, the ultimate, because he, our God, is love. The greatest act of love in all creation is that act whereby the Son of God, become man, a part of our creation, offered to his Father and ours the greatest thing in all creation, his own human life. The supreme act of love, historically taking place on Calvary, abides ever in God's now, at the summit of all that is creation. All else that is in creation has its meaning and value only to the extent that it shares in and expresses in some way that act of love.

At the Supper, Jesus reached into God's eternal now and made that future act present as he set before his Apostles, in the sacramental form of bread and wine, his own body and blood, broken and shed, an offering of sacrificial love. The twelve could easily understand a sacrificial meal. The *Zebah Todah*, the sacrifice communion, a sacrifice in which a meal was shared with God, was a popular part of their worship. What was offered to God was shared, eaten, by the beneficiaries. Meal and sacrifice were one, meant to bring about a true communion.

The Master, taking an old ritual, made it new; completing an old covenant, he made a new one. Bringing to fullness all the symbolism of every sacrifice and ritual there had ever been among God's people, he reached forward into history and, from God's now, he brought to the supper room the reality of Calvary. He made Calvary, as it was in God's now, truly present there at that moment of time, and he made the Apostles fully one with it. He gave it to them in a *Zebah Todah*. And he told them to do exactly as he had done. They were to make a *memoria* of what he did on the night before he died, a ritual act that would reach into God's now and make historically present the very act of Calvary—his supreme act of sacrificial love— so that those present could have it then and there as a *Zebah Todah*, so that it could be totally and completely their sacrifice in a communion meal with him.

There would be an apparent difference. On Calvary he seemed to hang there alone, suspended between heaven and earth. But in fact his whole "body" was there. The Head did not act without the body. Everyone who would ever be baptized into Christ was there, one with him. And to the extent that they would be one with him in will, in self-giving love, they were one with him in the eternal now of God, then historically manifest, offering this supreme act of saving, sacrificial love.

At the *memoria*, the Mass, the body, the congregation, his people, a priestly people with their presider are gathered, and Christ seems to be present only in sacramental sign and artistic representation in the crucifix. But the *memoria* is of that one ultimate act ever present in God's eternal now, coming to be present in our historical now. The act is one—a sacrifice of love. The communion of love of this here-and-now historical community enters into and is one with Christ's historical act of sacrificial love, so that in the eternal now of God they are one. Wherever that act is brought forth by this *memoria*, this ritual instituted by Christ, the Mass, it includes not only his act of sacrificial love, but also the participating love of every one of his members, his body, who have entered by faithful love into communion with his act of love. The love we bring to today's *memoria* is present in every Mass that will ever be offered. It was present at the Supper in the upper room. It was present on Calvary when our Head offered it to the Father, one with his own total gift of love.

Calvary is ever present in God's eternal now and can be made present in any moment of time. The Supper is ever present in God's eternal now, one with Calvary, and can be made present at any moment of time. Our offering at the *memoria*, the Mass, is ever present in God's now, one with Calvary and the Supper, and is made present whenever and wherever in time and space Calvary and the Supper are made present by the *memoria*, the Mass. This is the reality of the participation of men and women baptized into the priesthood of Jesus Christ. Our love, however great or however little it be, enters into the sacrifice of the whole Christ, ever to be a part of it. I don't know what more powerful motive we could have for wanting to bring all the love we possibly can to our offering of the Mass. In this *Zebah Todah*, we enter into communion not only with God and Christ, but in Christ our God, through him and with him, we enter into communion with every other person (all the saints, all our forebears, all our loved ones who have gone before us) who ever has and ever will (our progeny from generation to generation, and all the saints to come) offer the *memoria*; in a special way with those gathered around the altar with us, but also with all those around the world: Mother Teresa in Calcutta, Pope John Paul in the Vatican, the priests in the slave camps of Siberia, and Oscar Romero as he is shot to death at the altar.

As the celebrant repeats these powerful words of our Master, "Do this in memory of me," he or the deacon exclaims: "The mystery of faith!" Indeed it is a mystery of faith. As Saint Paul wrote to the Corinthians:

> The hidden wisdom which we teach in our mysteries is the wisdom God has predestined to be for our glory before the ages began. It is a wisdom that none of the masters of this age has ever known, or they could not have crucified the Lord of Glory. We teach what Scripture speaks of as the things no eye has ever seen and no ear has heard, things beyond the mind of the human person, all that God has prepared for those who love him. These things God has revealed to us through this Spirit, for the Spirit reaches the depths of everything, even the depths of God . . . . The unspirited person does not receive anything of the Spirit of God; to him it all seems nonsense.

With openness and attentiveness to the Spirit we come to sense, to know in a deep experiential way, the power that is ours as baptized priestly people to bring healing redemption to the whole of humanity through our participation in the most sacred and sublime *memoria*, the Mass. With great joy, with an almost awed sense of what we are about, we gather with our sisters and brothers, our fellow priests, to do this in memory of him.

THE ROMAN TRADITION

Imperial Rome had declined. The Roman Empire in the West had become a thing of the past. Papal Rome was coming into its own. As Pope Gregory I (already called "the Great") moved along the Via Triumphalis and down the Corsica on New Year's Day, A.D. 600, the people turned out in great numbers to see not only a liturgical celebration, but a civic function. For it was the spiritual father of Rome, her bishop, who had met the Lombards outside the city and saved it from destruction. Now, more truly than ever, it was his city. Yet the long entry march that brought the saintly bishop and his clergy of every rank from the Lateran Palace to the Petrine Basilica was first and foremost a liturgical procession.

The Mass—as it was then popularly called after a couple of centuries of gradual evolution—that unfolded that morning in the beautiful Constantinian basilica on the Vatican Hill, would have been familiar to any Catholic who remembers the Mass as it was celebrated before the Second Vatican Council—with the exception of the wider use of Greek. Even to this day, readings at papal Masses are in both Latin and Greek. By the time of Pope Gregory, after a long and difficult struggle beginning in the third century with the antipope Hippolytus, the liturgical language of Greek had been replaced by Latin, the vernacular of the people. Greek had been the language of the first Roman Christians and it had long remained the language of the educated. The Fathers of the Church wrote in Greek until the Africans, especially Saint Augustine (and his friend in Milan, Saint Ambrose), began to use Latin. Popes Leo the Great and Gregory regularized its use. Teaching is for the people; the liturgy belongs to the people of God. It must be their language. (Happily, the transition today from liturgical Latin to the vernacular of the people, while long overdue, has come with relative peace and facility.)

Although the liturgical Greek and some other aspects of the seventh-century ritual would have been unfamiliar to today's Roman Catholics, once the Pope began to pray the Eucharistic Prayer, the words would have been completely familiar, for they were the very words we use today in the first Eucharistic Prayer, called quite rightly the Roman Canon. The lists of saints commemorated, although today the priest is free to omit many of the names, are, after the Apostles, the saints of Rome: the early Popes and martyrs, men and women—Linus, Cletus, Clement, Sixtus, Cornelius, Cyprian, Lawrence, Chrysogonus, John and Paul, Cosmas and Damian, Alexander, Marcellinus, Peter, Felicity, Perpetua, Agatha, Lucy, Agnes, Cecilia, Anastasia—most of whose tombs are still popularly venerated in the holy city.

From the time of Pope Gregory I to the time of Pope John XXIII—more than thirteen and a half centuries—this prayer remained unchanged, daily prayed by countless bishops and priests with their people in all parts of an expanding world Church. In 1960, the piety of an audacious Pope, a man of history, who knew well that his earliest predecessors freely composed their own Eucharistic Prayers to suit the occasion, added the name of Saint Joseph to the Roman Canon. This little change, which shook up a very settled liturgical life in most parts of the world, was the nose of the camel butting under the tent flap—to use a not particularly eloquent analogy.

Many changes were to come, but for the most part the ancient and revered prayer remained intact. It suffered another minor change, but one touching its very heart and reminding us that even what was considered the most central and sacred part of the prayer, the words of institution, were the product of evolution and open to further evolution. The words "the mystery of faith" were taken out of what we have referred to as the words of consecration and are proclaimed after them to call forth the assent of the people.

We do not know exactly what words our Lord used when he presented the bread-flesh and the cup of wine-blood to his twelve. Saint Paul, who first wrote of the Supper, has one formula; the three Synoptic Gospels each offer their own. The particular formula that came to be enshrined in the Roman Canon and is used in all the other canons in the Roman rite differs from all of these scriptural texts as well as from the many different formulas used in the other rites in the Church. It is not the words that are sacrosanct; it is not a question of a magic formula. Under the impetus of a more scientific or rational approach to theology and Church practice during the scholastic dominance, there was a tendency or even a need to pin down the precise moment when the bread and wine were changed and the sacrifice of Calvary made present in the Mass. Today I think we realize that this "mystery of faith" lies essentially in a sacramental and effective *memoria* rather than in a formula.

A few other differences would have struck us if we had been among the crowd of worshipers that New Year's Day, A.D. 600. We would have noticed not only that we could not hear the Pope as he prayed the Eucharistic

Prayer, but that he went on with the prayer while we, or the choir, sang the *Sanctus*, the "Holy, holy, holy." Several factors came into play to produce this situation. There is the factor of the *arcana*—the practice of keeping the central mysteries of faith from the uninitiated. Perhaps this was in response to popular charges that Christians engaged in bloody sacrifices, even eating human flesh and drinking human blood. In the earliest Eucharistic assemblies the catechumens, those preparing for baptism, were asked to leave after the Liturgy of the Word with its instruction. Only the baptized faithful remained to offer the holy sacrifice, in virtue of their participation in the priesthood of Christ, and to eat the divine food. When the Church went public after the conversion of Emperor Constantine, the dismissal of the catechumens remained a part of the ritual, as it does in the East to this day. But in fact there was no sure way to sort out the large crowds in immense churches, and Masses were very much civic as well as religious functions. In the East, the sanctuary became an enclosed space, like the court of the priests in Jerusalem's Temple, and a veil was drawn over the entrance. The priest prayed his prayers quietly within while the people or choir went on with their chants outside. Pope Gregory had spent some years in Constantinople. Perhaps he brought this custom back to Rome. However, there was another factor involved, and this was the increased size of the basilicas and churches and the assemblies of the people participating in the Mass. Without modern methods of amplification, the celebrant could be heard only by those surrounding the altar. But all could participate in the singing, or at least hear the large choirs. So the priest quietly went on with his prayers.

With today's public-address systems, the Pope's voice can reach every corner of even the greatly enlarged baroque Saint Peter's, as well as vast congregations on the Boston Commons or in the fields of Iowa. Technology enables the celebrant to pray the great prayer in such a way that all in whose name he prays as president can immediately follow his every word, and with full cognizance endorse it with their "amen."

We are mindful, too, that this prayer is not only a prayer; it is also a proclamation. The priest does not repeat the story of the institution in detail in order to remind the Father, to whom he is addressing himself. While he with the assembly is objectively making *memoria* in response to the Lord's instruction, the narrative is meant also to call forth our faith and enliven our memories, so that our subjective dispositions may be fully in harmony with the objective reality. We need to hear again the word of faith so that we can be called forth and wholeheartedly proclaim this mystery of faith. In Pope Gregory's great basilica, there was no possibility for all to hear his voice. They could, however, hear the singing and become a part of its proclamation. So the choir sang on and they joined in.

Another mode of proclamation did develop, however, not in Rome but over the mountains in Gaul. It found its way across the Alps and became a part of our Roman rite. At Pope Gregory's New Year's Mass we would have missed the elevation of the host and chalice during the narration of the institution. He would have lifted them up in an offering gesture only at the conclusion of the Eucharistic Prayer.

Again, several factors contributed to the incorporation of this visible, symbolic mode of proclamation. Historically, the primary factor was heresy. When heretics began to deny that the words of institution brought about the Real Presence of Christ-God in the host and chalice, the consecrated species were held up to give the faithful a chance to proclaim their belief in a manifest act of adoration.

At the same time the unfortunate practice of rarely receiving the bread and wine in Holy Communion was gaining full acceptance in both the East and the West. But the pious wanted at least to see the Gift of the Lord. If they could not respond to his command to "Take and eat," they could at least feast on him with their eyes.

Modern liturgists tend to look upon the elevations of the host and chalice as interrupting the narration of the institution. I do not think this is necessarily so. Certainly, when Jesus took the matzah, gave thanks, broke it, and said, "Take, eat, this is my body," he handed it out to his twelve. There was a space of silence for them to hear what he said and to let the awesomeness of it sink in. The powerful visual and symbolic proclamation of holding the host and then the chalice aloft for a moment gives our faith a chance to be called forth more fully and respond more completely. The celebrant who effectively sets the host before us for a moment of silent, challenging presence is more integrally narrating the institution and proclaiming the mystery. We are being given the opportunity to let it penetrate to the depths of our being so that our whole being can respond. Thomas's "My Lord and my God" might spontaneously burst forth from our hearts. But even these words, or any other articulation of our faith and love, might be too much of a distraction at this moment. The celebrant did say: "This *is* my body"—this which our eyes behold is the very body of the Lord, the risen Lord. It is he, risen and alive, all glorious, albeit hidden in sacramental form. It is his *body*, his physical body, his whole body, his mystical body. We are all there. The living Head is never separated from his body. And he said, "This is *my* body." In some special way he is now truly present in our celebrant. He personally speaks to us, in challenging proclamation and command: "Take and eat, this is my body, *which will be given up for you. This is the cup of my blood. . . . It will be shed for you.*" We need time at each Eucharist to hear this proclamation and be present to it. That the president takes time to hold the bread and the cup before us and give us time to look upon them is no interruption. It responds to a deep need we have as a faithful and loving people. After these moments of silent encounter, we are better prepared to proclaim this mystery of faith.

A very stable tradition has come to us in the Roman Canon. Because of this it remains the favorite of many of the faithful. Some even prefer to hear it proclaimed in the traditional Latin—they are sufficiently familiar with the meaning of the words so that the Latin does not hinder the effectiveness of the proclamation, and they respond to the many emotional overtones and other connotations of the ancient language. Those who have such a preference may be a relatively small minority, but there is room for them among us. We can all profit from an occasional experience of the Latin celebration, which plunges us experientially into the roots of our tradition. It is good to know that we are a well-rooted and closely bonded people, enlivened by a consistent flow of life through centuries, a flow that has been received, enriched, and passed on by countless saints.

If the Roman Canon, Eucharistic Prayer I, has a special power to put us in touch with the tradition, it is not the only expression of it. Eucharistic Prayers II and IV bring to us even older elements of the Christian Eucharistic tradition, and Prayer III reminds us that this rich and varied tradition can ever be expressed in new ways.

EUCHARISTIC PRAYER I

The Roman Canon

We come to you, Father,
with praise and thanksgiving,
through Jesus Christ your Son.
Through him we ask you to accept and bless
these gifts we offer you in sacrifice.

We offer them for your holy catholic Church,
watch over it, Lord, and guide it;
grant it peace and unity throughout the world.
We offer them for John Paul, our Pope,
for our bishop,
and for all who hold and teach the catholic faith
that comes to us from the apostles.

Remember, Lord, your people,
especially those for whom we now pray.
Remember all of us gathered here before you.
You know how firmly we believe in you
and dedicate ourselves to you.
We offer you this sacrifice of praise
for ourselves and those who are dear to us.
We pray to you, our living and true God
for our well-being and redemption.

In union with the whole Church
we honor Mary,
the ever-virgin mother of Jesus Christ our Lord and God.
We honor Joseph, her husband,
the apostles and martyrs
Peter and Paul, Andrew,
James, John, Thomas, James, Philip,
Bartholomew, Matthew, Simon and Jude;
we honor Linus, Cletus, Clement, Sixtus,
Cornelius, Cyprian, Lawrence, Chrysogonus,
John and Paul, Cosmas and Damian
and all the saints.
May their merits and prayers
gain us your constant help and protection.
through Christ our Lord. Amen.

Father, accept this offering
from your whole family.
Grant us your peace in this life,
save us from final damnation,
and count us among those you have chosen.
Through Christ our Lord. Amen.

Bless and approve our offering;
make it acceptable to you,
an offering in spirit and in truth.
Let it become for us
the body and blood of Jesus Christ,
your only Son, our Lord.
Through Christ our Lord. Amen.

The day before he suffered
he took bread in his sacred hands

and looking up to heaven,
to you, his almighty Father,
he gave you thanks and praise.
He broke the bread,
gave it to his disciples, and said:
Take this, all of you, and eat it:
this is my body which will be given up for you.

When supper was ended,
he took the cup.
Again he gave you thanks and praise,
gave the cup to his disciples, and said:
Take this, all of you, and drink from it:
this is the cup of my blood,
the blood of the new and everlasting covenant.
It will be shed for you and for all
so that sins may be forgiven.
Do this in memory of me.

Let us proclaim the mystery of faith:
    Christ has died,
    Christ is risen,
    Christ will come again.

Father, we celebrate the memory of Christ, your Son.
We, your people and your ministers,
recall his passion,
his resurrection from the dead,
and his ascension into glory;
and from the many gifts you have given us
we offer to you, God of glory and majesty,
this holy and perfect sacrifice:
the bread of life
and the cup of eternal salvation.
Look with favor on these offerings
and accept them as once you accepted
the gifts of your servant Abel,
the sacrifice of Abraham, our father in faith,
and the bread and wine offered by your priest
    Melchisedech.
Almighty God,
we pray that your angel may take this sacrifice

to your altar in heaven.
Then, as we receive from this altar
the sacred body and blood of your Son,
let us be filled with every grace and blessing.
Through Christ our Lord. Amen.

Remember, Lord, those who have died
and have gone before us marked with the sign of
    faith,
especially those for whom we now pray.
May these, and all who sleep in Christ,
find in your presence
light, happiness, and peace.
Through Christ our Lord. Amen.

For ourselves, too, we ask
some share in the fellowship of your apostles and
    martyrs,
with John the Baptist, Stephen, Matthias, Barnabas,
Ignatius, Alexander, Marcellinus, Peter,
Felicity, Perpetua, Agatha, Lucy,
Agnes, Cecilia, Anastasia
and all the saints.
Though we are sinners,
we trust in your mercy and love.
Do not consider what we truly deserve,
but grant us your forgiveness.

Through Christ our Lord
you give us all these gifts.
You fill them with life and goodness,
you bless them and make them holy.

Through him,
with him,
in him,
in the unity of the Holy Spirit,
all glory and honor is yours,
almighty Father,
forever and ever.

   Amen.

THE PRAYER OF OUR MEDIATOR

❦ ❦ ❦

I peered through the hole in the farthest wall of the frescoed burial chamber. It was the feast of Saint Domitilla and we had been allowed to descend on our own into the catacombs that bear her name. For some hours we had been exploring the various subterranean galleries, fascinated not only by the richly decorated alcoves and family chambers (how amazingly fresh and bright the colors are after so many centuries), but by the seemingly endless rows of simple graves lining the walls from floor to roof. In a large chamber, undoubtedly the burial vault of a wealthy family, the frescoes depicted Eucharistic scenes: loaves and fishes, grapevines, the Last Supper. There was damage where robbers had searched for buried valuables, especially a large gapping hole at the end of the vault.

As I peered through this hole, I beheld a vision. Acolytes with burning torches and long tunics processed along another gallery, their flickering tapers lighting the way. They were followed by deacons in rich brocade dalmatics and, finally, a cardinal, his scarlet cassock and fine lace rochette visible in the opening of a heavy, rigid gold cope. My vision was undoubtedly a reality—a cardinal on his way to lead a festal service in some corner of the catacombs. But the sight carried me back across the centuries.

It was the third century. The Christian community had grown in Rome and Peter's succcessors had become noted figures in the Church. But the Bishop of Rome was also at times a hunted figure, especially during the more brutal persecutions. At such times it was not possible for him and his flock to gather safely in homes, even the homes of the more prominent and powerful citizens, to celebrate the Lord's Supper, and so the Pontiff descended into the expanding network of Christian catacombs. One day the venerable Pontiff Hippolytus sensed the pressure of mounting danger. The persecutors had on more than one occasion penetrated into these sacred depths, violating the commonly accepted sanctuary of the place of the dead, to seize their victims. The celebration of the Eucharist would

51

be brief, the high priest's prayer short, so they could quickly disperse. Short, but complete, and powerful in its intensity.

The Canon of Saint Hippolytus, who eventually was seized and courageously grasped the martyr's crown, has come down to us, even in its post-Vatican II renewed form, as a very short anaphora. Yet it is complete and powerful if prayed with its due intensity. Let us take a look at this canon, for in its brevity the details of the Eucharistic prayer stand out clearly.

EUCHARISTIC PRAYER II

Based on the Anaphora attributed to Saint Hippolytus

Lord, you are holy indeed,
the fountain of all holiness.

(EPICLESIS)
Let your Spirit come upon these gifts to make them holy,
so that they may become for us
the body and blood of our Lord, Jesus Christ.

(NARRATIVE)
Before he was given up to death,
a death he freely accepted,
he took bread and gave you thanks.
He broke the bread,
gave it to his disciples, and said:
Take this, all of you, and eat it:
this is my body which will be given up for you.

When supper was ended, he took the cup.
Again he gave you thanks and praise,
gave the cup to his disciples, and said:
Take this, all of you, and drink from it:
this is the cup of my blood,
the blood of the new and everlasting covenant.
It will be shed for you and for all
so that sins may be forgiven.
Do this in memory of me.

Let us proclaim the mystery of faith:

(ACCLAMATION)
> *Dying you destroyed our death,*
> *rising you restored our life.*
> *Lord Jesus, come in glory.*

(ANAMNESIS)
In memory of his death and resurrection,
we offer you, Father, this life-giving bread,
this saving cup.
We thank you for counting us worthy
to stand in your presence and serve you.
May all of us who share in the body and blood of Christ
be brought together in unity by the Holy Spirit.

(INTERCESSIONS)
Lord, remember you Church throughout the world;
make us grow in love,
together with John Paul, our Pope,
our bishop, and all the clergy.

Remember our brothers and sisters
who have gone to their rest
in the hope of rising again;
bring them and all the departed
into the light of your presence.

(COMMEMORATIONS)
Have mercy on us all;
make us worthy to share eternal life
with Mary, the virgin Mother of God,
with the apostles, and with all the saints
who have done your will throughout the ages.
May we praise you in union with them,
and give you glory
through your Son, Jesus Christ.

(DOXOLOGY)
Through him,
with him,
in him,
in the unity of the Holy Spirit,

all glory and honor is yours,
almighty Father,
for ever and ever.

(ACCLAMATION)
  Amen.

The acclamation "Holy, holy, holy," just sung by the people, is taken up by the priest, the mediator, who comes from the people to the Father. In the three other Eucharistic Prayers—the Roman (I), the new (III), and the Basilian (IV)—the priest opens with the name Father. Here in Prayer II it is Lord, but there is no doubt that he is speaking to the Father. The people have just proclaimed the Father's holiness, and the priest affirms this and relates it back to the people. You are holy—the fountain of holiness—the source of the people's holiness. And he asks this source to pour itself out now upon the people's gift.

This invocation of the Holy Spirit (called in Greek the *epiclesis*) was placed before the words of institution in all the Western canons as the result of a controversy in the early Church. Eastern Christians, so conscious that the consecration and transubstantiating change of the bread and wine into the body and blood of Jesus could only come about by the power of God, and that God works among us through his Holy Spirit, asserted that the sacrificial change took place only after the invocation of the Spirit, which the Eastern anaphoras place after the words of institution. Western theologians held that the recitation of the words of institution fulfilled Christ's command to "Do this in memory of me," and, hence, this was the operative moment.

We need not spend time here rehearsing the whole sad controversy. It is this prayer in its wholeness that we want to concentrate on, entering into the full sacrificial love of the Son to the Father for all. The Spirit, with the Father and the Son, is operative, as the divine persons in their one power effect all that is effected.

The words of institution are central in this *memoria*, and this brief canon wastes no time in getting to them. While there is some variety in their immediate contexts, the words of institution are identical in all the Western anaphoras. Pope Paul VI insisted on this in order that, at this sacred moment, the priest would be most familiar with the text and would be able to give it his fullest attention. This meant a modification in the formula of the Roman Canon, consonant with the introduction of the proclamation of faith which is found in all four canons immediately after the words of institution.

This is the only place in the Western canons apart from those approved for children's Masses where the people break into the prayer of the celebrant. It is something that has been introduced with the renewal and conforms to the more ancient practice that has always prevailed in the East. In the Byzantine liturgies both sections of the words of institution are greeted with the brief acclamation: "Amen." The people also break in with a hymn to the Holy Mother of God and other brief responses. In other liturgies, such responses are more numerous. This is especially true, and beautifully so, in the experimental liturgies used in India. (In Appendix B you will find a text of such a liturgy.)

After the words of institution and the acclamation, the name of Father (this time in all the canons) is again on the lips of the priest. There is a conscious reflection that this is a *memoria*, fulfilling Christ's command; it is now offered to the Father in thanksgiving, *eucharistia*.

The fruit of the offering is sought, first for those present, then for the whole Church with its pastors. The fourth canon is the only one that explicitly reaches beyond the Church or the faithful to "all who seek you [the Lord] with a sincere heart." As is clearly stated in the narrative of the institution, this sacrifice was offered for all.

The anaphora then prays for the departed, allowing in this canon for a special commemoration of particular deceased. The third canon also allows for this, with an even fuller and more beautiful formula. The Roman Canon keeps its centuries-long rigidity and allows only a silent pause. The Basilian anaphora makes no such provision. This seems surprising in that the Byzantine liturgies do allow for the introduction of a special litany for the deceased. However, this litany is outside the anaphora and would be more relative to our Prayer of the Faithful. So the absence of an alternate text in the fourth canon is consonant with its origin.

Finally, there is a commemoration of those who have already received the full benefit of the Mass, the saving sacrifice of our Lord. These are his fruits, these are his glory; first of all, Mary, then his chosen band of disciples, and then all the rest. We ask to be one with them.

Each of the four canons has these intercessions and commemorations, but they arrange them differently. The new canon (III), like the older canons of Hippolytus and Basil, places both of these after the constitutive elements—the narration of the institution; the *epiclesis*, or invocation of the Spirit; and the *anamnesis*, or *memoria*—but it inverts the order and places the commemorations before the intercessions. In this it corresponds more to the Anaphora of Saint Basil than does the Basilian adaptation (IV). The Roman Canon seeks a balance, and puts the intercessions for the living Church and the primary commemoration, along with the *epiclesis*, before the narrative, which it sees as central. The *anamnesis*, with the intercession for the deceased and secondary commemorations, is placed after the narrative.

All four canons come to the same resounding conclusion in an identical doxology, which, in a literal translation of the Latin, comes out grammatically incorrect in English. One of the things that makes it difficult for many priests to appropriate the canons and pray them as their own is the translations. A certain amount of reflection and meditation can enable the priest as a man of faith to enter into the rich theology these prayers reflect, a glorious reality of communion in the saving passion of Christ. He may come to identify with one more than another, or he may see merit in experiencing the interconnections differently in the different canons on succeeding days, so that his insight will be constantly enriched. But faith and devotion will not, and are not meant to, enable one to identify with awkward English, poor phrasing, and bad grammar. The celebrant will want to pray the reality of these prayers as authentically as he can, being as fully there as he can, so that the people can be there with him.

While more acclamations during the anaphora might be a desirable addition—they might well arise spontaneously within a charismatic assembly—it does not seem at all desirable to change the intercessions of the priestly prayer into a "prayer of the faithful." That has its own place. However, when the priest, the mediator, prays the intercessions he should be mindful of the deepest concerns of the praying assembly, whether these were made known through the prayer of the faithful or otherwise. The special insertions for the intercessions for the deceased in the Canon of Saint Hippolytus and the new canon pattern this. But it is time for the priest to pray for the people rather than for them to join in with their petitions. If the liturgical service has moved along the way it should have, the people will feel confident that their mediator, one with Jesus before the Father, is powerfully carrying their concerns forward in Christ. They will support his prayer with participative silence and fitting acclamation. Their final amen will be a great amen, an amen that sums up all that they are, their whole redeemed and divinized being to the Father through and with and in the Son, in that unity who is our common Spirit, the Divine Love: Amen.

The anaphora is the priest's prayer, the mediator's prayer. The people, for whom he is mediating at this moment, want the priest to be truly praying. It is not the time for proclamation, for speaking to the people. It is the time for speaking to God—speaking to God loudly and clearly enough so that those for whom he is speaking can hear what he is saying for them, and add "amen." It is an advantage if the priest can so assimilate this prayer that he can pray it without having to read it. But we are not all gifted with the ability to do this. The more important thing is for the priest to have so assimilated this prayer that it is truly his prayer, whether it is said from memory or read from a book.

I have sometimes wondered whether some priests have ever spent any time with the prayer of the anaphora outside of the time they have read it at the altar. It can hardly be a deep prayer welling up from within the priest's heart if he has not made it his own by hours of reflection and very personal communion with the Father about each of the theological realities and attitudes that he expresses in the anaphora. For it to be a powerful and empowering prayer, subjectively as well as objectively, when he prays it standing before the people, the priest needs to have made each of its elements a part of his own inner attitude through his hidden prayer to the Father. A priest cannot limit himself to being priest-mediator only when he is standing at the altar: he must be so in the fabric of his consecrated being. He is a man taken from among men for this. The Mass is the high point of his mediatorial activity. The celebrations of the other sacraments are most significant moments. But his whole life is to be one of mediation. His words of counsel and his presence are to be a constant mediation of God's love, and a receiving of his people and their love, joy, sorrow, and pain for the Father. Especially is he to devote a generous portion of his time and a fullness of heart to compassionate mediatorial prayer. It is only in the context of a full attitude and life of mediation that a priest can truly pray his priestly prayer at the Mass in a way that will call forth from the people a wholehearted, empowered "Amen!"

True, the priest is a man—drawn from among men, yet still in the midst of men and women—still a man needing all the support that any man needs. He needs the support of affirmation and accountability. When a priest is obviously striving truly to pray for the people in this great prayer, his effort should be supported and affirmed not only by a very attentive presence to him during his prayer and a responsive amen at the end of it, but also by expressions of appreciation after Mass and at other times. I don't think we should take anyone for granted, even though our Lord did say: "When you have done all this you ought then to say: 'I am an unprofitable servant.'" To go on faithfully fulfilling their service, priests need support and affirmation.

And if we priests are not fulfilling our service we need to be called to account. Positive criticism is far more helpful than negative. In one way, negative criticism is easier—to point out what is wrong, what is lacking, is easier than to come up with a positive suggestion for a remedy. However, where there is love and compassion it is certainly easier to offer constructive suggestions and expectations than negative evaluations. It is not easy for most parishioners to speak frankly to their priests. Even if the priest waits at the door to receive them as they go out, it is easier to offer some platitude and pass on than to offer some authentic critique.

A good priest's generosity and goodness as a person can and should always be affirmed; a positive word of encouragement can be added, a suggestion or the expression of a hope or expectation can call him forth to something better. If we are not satisfied with the way our priest leads us at the Eucharist, the way our mediator prays for us, all the blame is not to be laid at his door. We have our responsibility to call him forth, to support him, to affirm him, to urge him on, to make him accountable. If we want a true and powerful mediator in our priest—and deep down we all do—we need to take responsibility for him. We need to let him know we want this of him and support him by our prayers for him, by our words and actions of encouragement, by our support when he is doing it, by our expressions of appreciation and gratitude when he has done it, and by letting him know when we sense he has failed us. He is "Father"; he is also brother and friend, one with us in Christ. Let us be fully involved with our mediator in his prayer, and in his life, which is the essential context of that prayer.

SOMETHING NEW

They flowed out through the great bronze doors, hundreds and hundreds of them, rank upon rank, and slowly made their way through Bernini's columns, past the masses packed in the enormous square, up the gentle steps, and into the patriarchal basilica of Saint Peter. Never before had so many mitred heads been gathered together in one place. They came from every continent and nation, from every race and people. At the end came the "old man" who had ended up "at the top of the heap." And today he knew it, and the entire world knew it, as never before. It was the opening of the Second Vatican Council, October 11, 1962; Pope John XXIII, the head, had summoned the College of Bishops from all the corners of the earth. That morning we would experience the Mass as the prayer of the Church in a most special way.

In the late afternoon, after the siesta, I walked along the winding Tiber River, through Trastevere, over the bridge, and up the sharp embankment called the Aventino—one of the seven hills of Rome, just inside Saint Paul's Gate. On its summit, with a maginificent view past the Genniculum to Saint Peter's, stood the relatively new Benedictine International College, Sant' Anselmo. I had come this afternoon to see an old friend, Dom Cyprian Vagaggini, a delightful monk with an almost cherubic face, a shaven head, and eyes sparkling with keen curiosity and a deep peaceful joy. After his ordination Dom Cyprian had dedicated about five years to biblical studies, then he went on to the Fathers and, after some years with them, to the scholastics. He was ready to enter fully into Aquinas's great *Summa* because he came to it with the same rich background as the Angelic Doctor himself. He again spent about five years with scholastic theology, readying himself for that which he always saw to be the consummation of all this study: the liturgy. He had recently published what may well be the most significant book of the liturgical renewal, *The Theological Dimensions of the Liturgy*. Dom Cyprian was well prepared to serve the ecumenical council as a *peritus*, an "expert." It was in his capacity as an expert that I approached him on this particular afternoon. The first session of the council was to be dedicated in large part to a constitution on the liturgy. I wanted to get more in touch with the man who was behind it, a monk who seemed to have the fullest grasp of the reality of worship—that all the Church's learning, all her teaching had little value, made little sense, if it did not culminate in living worship. And that worship would be what it should be only if it were a true expression of the people of God as we here and now exist on our pilgrimage. We come out of a long tradition, reaching back to the Creation and to the Creator himself. All that heritage is incarnate in us and should be in our liturgy. The pilgrim Church is one with the glorious Church in heaven. And that should be expressed in our liturgy. Grasping the full reality of what is, liturgy will have to be ever new and renewing. For tradition is living; the Church is ever growing.

A short time before, Pope John XXIII had had the "audacity" to add Saint Joseph's name to the Roman Canon, the one Eucharistic Prayer used in most of the West and verbally unchanged for centuries. In fact, seminarians were being taught that it was a mortal sin to change a single word of the canon when saying Mass. Pope John's audacity sent a tremor, or was it an out and out quake, through the whole Church. For some it was a quake of joy, for others of terror. It presaged things to come. Would the Church be ready? What could we hope for? What could we do to prepare for it? These were the questions that I brought to the Aventino that historic day.

The Church had quaked at a few words being added in Latin to the sacrosanct anaphora. Even then, Dom Cyprian, knowing what was inevitably to come and seeking to use the gifts and opportunities God had given him to guide the Church's course wisely and richly, was preparing a new Eucharistic Prayer. He was drawing from Alexandrian, Byzantine, and Maronite anaphoras, and even from Gallican liturgy. It would be richly traditional, but it would be new. The fruit of his labors blossomed in Eucharistic Prayer III.

Unlike the second and fourth, which are directly drawn from early anaphoras, the third prayer is new. Now it is probably the most popular of the Eucharistic Prayers. This may be because it is closest to the familiar Roman Canon, but shorter, clearer, and simpler. Like the first prayer, it does not have a preface of its own but is open to incorporating any of the expanding repertoire of seasonal, festive, and occasional prefaces that are available. Its beautiful amplification of the intercession for the deceased makes it the chosen Eucharistic Prayer for funerals and other Masses for the dead.

This new prayer brings to the fore the role of the Holy Spirit, through creation and salvation history, in the gathering of a godly people *from east to west*. He is called upon not only to sanctify the Church's offering but also to fill the offerers, making them *one body, one spirit in Christ*. This emphasis on the role of the Spirit has made this the favorite Eucharistic Prayer among charismatic groups, where participants are especially aware of his role in their lives and in the life of the Church and the sanctification of the world. It is also more appropriate for ecumenical use inasmuch as Eastern Christians have always been surprised at the absence of the explicit invocation of the Holy Spirit in the Western anaphora.

This third Eucharistic Prayer is closest to the Roman Canon among the new prayers, yet it does represent a significant shift in perspective. The Christology and ecclesiology inspiring the first prayer is largely that of the Epistle to the Hebrews. The sacrifice of the New Covenant is the fulfillment of the Old, the new High Priest penetrates the true holy of holies in heaven and offers the one perduring sacrifice. The new prayer draws more from the reconciliation theology of Saint Paul's Epistle to the Colossians. It expresses well the relation between the Church's offering and Christ's: *Look with favor on your Church's offering, and see the Victim whose death has reconciled us to yourself.* It is more cosmic, it is more in this cosmos. Some fear that the liturgy has lost much of its transcendence, its mystery. But there is mystery in the immanent. If it has moved from projecting the mystery out there beyond the signs and symbols to finding it with us, the community, isn't this more challenging? And isn't this more in accord with the baptismal reality of who we are who have been baptized into Christ—*I live, now not I but Christ lives in me?* Is this not more in accord with the nature of the Church, of the Christian community? Christ identifies with us, his Spirit enlivens us, we offer now his sacrifice as ours to be sanctified by his Spirit and carry on the work of his redemption.

Quiet, prayerful reflection on this Eucharistic Prayer, pursuing the biblical and theological dimensions, will reveal to us more and more of its richness, enable us to draw more and more from it, and help us to pray it ever more fully.

EUCHARISTIC PRAYER III

Father, you are holy indeed,
and all creation rightly gives you praise.
All life, all holiness comes from you
through your Son, Jesus Christ our Lord,
by the working of the Holy Spirit.
From age to age you gather a people to yourself,
so that from east to west
a perfect offering may be made
to the glory of your name.

And so, Father, we bring you these gifts.
We ask you to make them holy by the power of your Spirit,
that they may become the body and blood
of your Son, our Lord Jesus Christ,
at whose command we celebrate this eucharist.

On the night he was betrayed,
he took bread and gave you thanks and praise.
He broke the bread, gave it to his disciples, and said:
Take this, all of you, and eat it:
this is my body which will be given up for you.

When supper was ended, he took the cup.
Again he gave you thanks and praise,
gave the cup to his disciples, and said:
Take this, all of you, and drink from it:
this is the cup of my blood,
the blood of the new and everlasting covenant.
It will be shed for you and for all
so that sins may be forgiven.
Do this in memory of me.

Let us proclaim the mystery of faith:

> *When we eat this bread and drink this cup,*
> *we proclaim your death, Lord Jesus,*
> *until you come in glory.*

Father, calling to mind the death your Son endured for our salvation,
his glorious resurrection and ascension into heaven,
and ready to greet him when he comes again,
we offer you in thanksgiving this holy and living sacrifice.
Look with favor on your Church's offering,
and see the Victim whose death has reconciled us to yourself.
Grant that we, who are nourished by his body and blood,
may be filled with his Holy Spirit,
and become one body, one spirit in Christ.

May he make us an everlasting gift to you
and enable us to share in the inheritance of your saints,
with Mary, the virgin Mother of God;

with the apostles, the martyrs, and all the saints,
on whose constant intercession we rely for help.

Lord, may this sacrifice,
which has made our peace with you,
advance the peace and salvation of all the world.
Strengthen in faith and love your pilgrim Church on earth;
your servant, Pope John Paul, our bishop,
and all the bishops,
with the clergy and the entire people your Son has gained for you.
Father, hear the prayers of the family you have gathered here before you.
In mercy and love unite all your children wherever they may be.

Welcome into your kingdom our departed brothers and sisters,
and all who have left this world in your friendship.
We hope to enjoy for ever the vision of your glory,
through Christ our Lord, from whom all good things come.

Through him,
with him,
in him,
in the unity of the Holy Spirit,
all glory and honor is yours,
almighty Father,
for ever and ever.

Amen.

IN THE SPIRIT OF BYZANTIUM

❊ ❊ ❊

In the long silent pause one could concentrate on the rich blend of odors: the sweet mellow odor of beeswax, the pungent sweetness of Athonite incense, the earthy smell of olive oil, the homey smell of fresh-baked bread that activates the digestive fluids, and the fruity smell of sweet red wine. The whole atmosphere was charged with sacramental sensations: the flickering lamps catching the golds and silvers of the icons, the swinging lamps, the whirling chandeliers, the glittering brocade vestments—the eyes could be filled. And the ears had been filled, too, first with chants of rich voices and melodies, and then with the more powerful and evocative sounds of silence. The quiet, the calm, the peace—yet exhilaration and expectation, too—touch every pore of the body.

As I stood in the corner stall in the rear of the *katolicon*, the main church of the Byzantine monastery of Stavronikita, I was aware of all these sensations, and yet not aware of them. All concentration was focused on the figure, hidden behind the veil and gates, and with him and in him, on that which is truly beyond. Suddenly his voice, peaceful yet powerful, with the richness and depth of a manly sweetness, solemn, sacred:

> Take, eat; this is my body, which is broken for you for
> the remission of sins.
> Amen.

> Drink of this, all of you, this is my blood of the New
> Testament, which is shed for you and for many for the
> remission of sins.
> Amen.

> We offer you your own, from what is your own, in all
> and for the sake of all.

Silence again embraced the church. Only the slightest rustle of vestments indicated that the celebrant and his concelebrants had prostrated themselves before the presence of the saving Lord. And we all did likewise, our foreheads to the marble floor, our hearts open and poured out.

Then the silent prayer continued.

My thoughts went back to the great Jerusalem Temple, the vast crowds standing in silent awe while the high priest entered the holy of holies to offer incense before the Most High; I thought of those who stood in growing expectation and wonder while the aged priest Zacharius delayed at the evening incense. Yes, an angel was speaking to him.

The priest-mediator is a part of our heritage. "Every high priest has been taken from among the people and is appointed to act for men and women in their relation with God, to offer gifts and sacrifices for sins." We are very conscious of our sins. We want someone to stand in our stead, someone with pull. We have Christ, our great high priest, who ascended the cross and pleaded before the Father with blood far more eloquent than the blood of any other sacrifice. He continues now to make intercession for us. But knowing our very human need to experience his presence and mediation incarnationally, he has established a ministerial priesthood, calling forth men and ordaining them to stand in his stead. In this most holy time of the Mass, when our passing time is intersected by his eternity, he stands as a man in our midst and speaks for us to the Father.

I always tell those who kindly invite me to visit them that I never forget an invitation; they may find me responding when they least expect it. Some years ago the spiritual director of Immaculate Conception Seminary invited me to use their facilities: "Come any time. Just call us up and we will meet you at the airport." As it happened, a few weeks later my plane schedule was delayed by winter storms and I found that I would be arriving in New York at two o'clock in the morning. "Just call." I did. And, true to his word, they came.

That day I was invited to offer Mass for the seminarians. Concelebration had not yet been re-established, but the altar had been turned around to face the congregation. After lunch I had an informal rap session with the deacons. One of them remarked, "You know, your Mass was different." I summoned up my courage and replied, "How so?" The deacon replied, "You really spoke to the Father."

In the old days, when the priest ascended the altar, going up and away from the people, it was easy for them to sense that he was entering into special communion with God in their behalf. Today as the priest stands in the midst of the assembly, face to face with the people, they can quickly sense whether he is really speaking to the Father. The priest will not be able to do this unless he also and frequently goes to his room, closes the door, and communes with his Father in secret. This is what the people want and should be able to expect from their priests, whose call they respect and whose lives they support.

Having the altar facing the people has perhaps engendered some confusion. During the Mass the priest does speak to the people much of the time. He proclaims the Gospel in the person of Christ. He calls them forth and directs their communal prayer. He prepares them for the great prayer as he leads them into the preface. Then there comes the time to speak to the other Party: "We come to you, Father." The great prayer, the anaphora or canon is addressed to the Father. And the priest should turn his attention to him.

I know a young priest, Father Don, who has committed this prayer to memory so that he may be free to forget even the book and be completely free to speak to the Father. He is a very prayerful young man, nourished by years in the charismatic movement and a year in a monastery. When he prays the Mass the people have no doubt that he does converse with the Father, his Father and theirs, the Father of our Lord Jesus Christ. At the end of the great prayer he will "return" to them. The preface of the Communion rite calls upon him to speak directly to them. But for the moment he is with the Father. And his congregation appreciates this—they like to attend his Mass. This is the way it should be. They don't feel left out, because as he prays, he prays loudly and clearly and distinctly, so they can hear and be part of the prayer, knowing he is speaking to the Father for them.

There is that one moment when the priest, if he does not have a deacon, breaks out of his prayer and calls forth the community: "Let us proclaim this mystery of faith." The Byzantine liturgy is richer in these moments of dialogue and acclamation—perhaps it needs to be, as the priest is still hidden in his silence within the sanctuary. Be that as it may, when Father Vasileios, after having prayed for

> all those who have fallen asleep before, in the hope of resurrection to eternal life . . . all orthodox bishops rightly dispensing the word of your truth, all the priests, the deacons in Christ and all the ranks of the clergy . . . your holy, catholic, and apostolic Church, which is from one end of the earth to the other . . . those who have offered you these holy gifts, and those for whom and through whom and on account of whom they offered them . . . those who bring forth good fruit and do good work in your holy Churches, and who care for the poor . . . those who are in deserts and mountains and in dens and caves of the earth . . . those who remain in virginity and continence and asceticism, and those who lead saintly lives in the world . . . our most faithful and pious public authorities whom you have counted worthy to be appointed over our land . . . all lawmakers and magistrates and our brethren in public office and in all the armed forces . . . the people here present and those who are absent for reasonable causes . . . babes . . . youths . . . elderly . . . the feebleminded . . . the scattered . . . the wandering . . . those who are bothered by unclean spirits . . . those at sea . . . travelers . . . widows . . . orphans . . . prisoners . . . the sick . . . those who stand before tribunals and those

in exile and in all kinds of tribulations and accidents and all who need
your great mercy; those who love us and those who hate us, and those
who have begged us, unworthy though we be, to remember them in our
prayers . . . all your people, O Lord our God . . . those we have omitted
through ignorance or forgetfulness or because of the multitude of their
names . . . this city and every city and country place . . . our holy Patriarch . . . our most reverend Bishop . . . all men and women,

emerged from his silence with the beautiful doxology:

and grant that with one mouth and one heart we may glorify and extol
your most noble and magnificent name of Father, Son, and Holy Spirit,
now and always and for ever and ever.

and blessed us:

And may the mercies of our great God and
Savior Jesus Christ be with you all.

I sensed deeply that this man of God had indeed been in the holy place
and touched God, bringing back to us his blessing.

In the early Church the canon was not fixed. It was the priest's prayer
and he was responsible to compose it himself. Whether this led to exag-
geration, or whether the average priest found it too difficult, in time set
formulas prevailed. The establishment of certain canons may also have
been due to a change from the situation where the Mass was usually led
by the bishop to one where his assistant priests would often offer Mass
apart from him for the growing and more dispersed segments of his flock.
In time, two or three canons came to prevail among Byzantine Christians: those of Saint John Chrysostom, Saint Basil (used ordinarily only
on his feast and the Sundays of Lent), and a pre-sanctified liturgy attrib-
uted to Basil's good friend Saint Gregory the Theologian (which is used
on weekdays in Lent). The latter is actually a Vesper office with a Communion service, such as we have in the West on Good Friday. In the West,
only one canon was retained, called the Roman Canon. With the renewal
after the Second Vatican Council, three other canons were added to this,
and then some others meant for more particular occasions. This gives the
priest a new freedom, and a new responsibility. He may choose to vary
the canon from day to day, especially if he is serving the same community
regularly. Some priests may find that this variety helps them to avoid the
deadening effects of routine. Or the priest may, like Father Don, make
one of these canons his own in a very deep way. Whatever choice he re-

sponsibly makes, as he enters into the canon of the Mass, it is time for the priest, with all the people gathered into his heart and his prayer, to speak to the Father.

EUCHARISTIC PRAYER IV

Based on the Anaphora attributed to Saint Basil the Great

(PREFACE)
Father in heaven,
it is right that we should give you thanks and glory:
you alone are God, living and true.
Through all eternity you live in unapproachable light.
Source of life and goodness, you have created all things,
to fill your creatures with every blessing
and lead all to the joyful vision of your light.
Countless hosts of angels stand before you to do your will;
they look upon your splendor
and praise you, night and day.
United with them,
and in the name of every creature under heaven,
we too praise your glory as we say:

(ACCLAMATION)
Holy, holy, holy Lord, God of power and might,
heaven and earth are full of your glory.
Hosanna in the highest.
Blessed is he who comes in the name of the Lord.
Hosanna in the highest.

(ANAPHORA)
Father, we acknowledge your greatness:
all your actions show your wisdom and love.
You formed us in your own likeness
and set us over the whole world
to serve you, our creator,
and to rule over all creatures.
Even when we disobeyed you and lost your friendship
you did not abandon us to the power of death,
but helped all to seek and find you.
Again and again you offered a covenant to us,

and through the prophets taught us to hope for salvation.
Father, you so loved the world
that in the fullness of time you sent your only Son to
    be our Savior.
He was conceived through the power of the Holy Spirit,
and born of the Virgin Mary,
a man like us in all things but sin.
To the poor he proclaimed the good news
    of salvation,
to prisoners, freedom,
and to those in sorrow, joy.
In fulfillment of your will
he gave himself up to death;
but by rising from the dead,
he destroyed death and restored life.
And that we might live no longer for ourselves but for him,
he sent the Holy Spirit from you, Father,
as his first gift to those who believe,
to complete his work on earth
and bring us the fullness of grace.

(EPICLESIS)
Father, may this Holy Spirit sanctify these offerings.
Let them become the body and blood of Jesus
    Christ our Lord
as we celebrate the great mystery
which he left us as an everlasting covenant.

(NARRATIVE)
He always loved those who were his own in the world.
When the time came for him to be glorified by you,
    his heavenly Father,
he showed the depth of his love.
While they were at supper,
he took bread, said the blessing, broke the bread
and gave it to his disciples, saying:
Take this, all of you, and eat it:
this is my body which will be given up for you.

In the same way, he took the cup, filled with wine.
He gave you thanks, and giving the cup to his
    disciples, said:

Take this, all of you, and drink from it:
this is the cup of my blood,
the blood of the new and everlasting covenant.
It will be shed for you and for all
so that sins may be forgiven.
Do this in memory of me.

Let us proclaim the mystery of faith:

(ACCLAMATION)
>   *Lord, by your cross and resurrection*
>   *you have set us free.*
>   *You are the Savior of the world.*

(ANAMNESIS)
Father, we now celebrate this memorial of our
   redemption.
We recall Christ's death, his descent among
   the dead,
his resurrection, and his ascension to your right hand;
and, looking forward to his coming in glory,
we offer you his body and blood,
the acceptable sacrifice
which brings salvation to the whole world.

Lord, look upon this sacrifice which you have
   given to your Church;
and by your Holy Spirit, gather all who share this
   bread and wine
into the one body of Christ, a living sacrifice of praise.

(INTERCESSIONS)
Lord, remember those for whom we offer this sacrifice,
especially John Paul, our Pope,
our bishop, and bishops and clergy everywhere.
Remember those who take part in this offering,
those here present and all your people,
and all who seek you with a sincere heart.
Remember those who have died in the peace of Christ
and all the dead whose faith is known to you alone.

(COMMEMORATIONS)
Father, in your mercy grant also to us, your children,
to enter into our heavenly inheritance
in the company of the Virgin Mary, the Mother of
    God,
and your apostles and saints.
Then, in your kingdom, freed from the corruption of
    sin and death,
we shall sing your glory with every creature through
    Christ our Lord,
through whom you give us everything that is good.

(DOXOLOGY)
Through him,
with him,
in him,
in the unity of the Holy Spirit,
all glory and honor is yours,
almighty Father,
for ever and ever.

(ACCLAMATION)
    Amen.

Appendix A includes the Anaphora of Saint Basil the Great so that you
can compare this Eucharistic Prayer with its source. If this prayer seems
much longer and richer than the other Eucharistic Prayers we are using
in the West, it is very short in comparison with the fullness of Saint Basil's
prayer.

True to its source, this particular canon is never to be separated from
its own invariable preface, which sweeps us up into the heavenly fulfillment of the salvation history that it will proclaim at length. Even if it is
shorn of the Byzantine splendor of the original, the account of salvation
history in this anaphora is quite complete, beginning with the Creation
and Fall, moving through the covenants with Noah, and with Abraham
and his descendants, to Sinai and the long line of prophets, to the fullness
of time. The full proclamation of the Good News in the life, death, and
resurrection of the Son and the coming of the Spirit place this *memoria* in
full context.

The shift of the *epiclesis* to interrupt the flow of salvation history in the narrative is in response to a Western theological—or perhaps, more truly, rubrical—concern. In its placement it contrasts with its source, but in its content it is very true to it. A strong emphasis on the Holy Spirit in a Basilian prayer is to be expected, for it was this Cappadocian Father who did much to help the Church elaborate its theology concerning the Third Person of the Blessed Trinity.

True to its Eastern origin, the *anamnesis* of this anaphora brings in an element not found in other Western canons—the descent among the dead. There is another inversion of order when the intercessions are placed before the commemorations, as in the Roman tradition found in Eucharistic Prayers I and II. This inversion seems hardly necessary, for in the new canon (III) the Byzantine order is followed. I do want to point out the richness of the Eastern commemoration of the Holy Mother of God: "Especially for our all holy, spotless, most highly blessed and glorious Lady, the Mother of God and ever-virgin Mary." This calls forth from the faithful an acclamation that is variable but usually takes this form:

> It is fitting and right to call you blessed, O Godbearer, you are ever-blessed and all-blameless and the Mother of our God. Higher in honor than the Cherubim and more glorious without compare than the Seraphim, you gave birth to God the Word in virginity. You are truly Mother of God; you do we magnify.

Because of its length and its invariable preface, the fourth Eucharistic Prayer tends to be used less frequently. This is understandable. However, I would like to suggest that it might be used at Saturday morning liturgies, when the community usually has more leisure at its disposal for celebration. And, in this connection, since Saturday is traditionally a day dedicated to Mary, recalling that Saturday when the whole faith of the Christian people rested in her heart, some of the beautiful Marian acclamations of the Eastern tradition (such as the ones given above and in the Anaphora of St. Basil in Appendix A) might be used by the people. At every Eucharist, in union with the whole Church, we commemorate, in the first place, the Holy Mother of God, knowing that the most sacred Victim we offer in sacrifice and all his fruits come to us through her. It is truly fitting and right to call her blessed. Her we do magnify.

LET THE CHILDREN COME

❧ ❧ ❧

A few years ago I was in Kalamazoo for a week, assisting in the establishment of the Institute of Cistercian Studies at Western Michigan University. On Sunday morning I took advantage of the opportunity to assist at the liturgy at the local Orthodox Church of Saints Helena and Constantine. I had on many occasions assisted at Byzantine liturgy in monasteries but this was the first time I had attended a parish liturgy. When the priest came forth through the Royal Doors with Holy Communion, few approached. This did not surprise me for the discipline and practice in regard to frequent Communion in the Orthodox Church is much the same as it was in the Roman Catholic Church prior to the renewals inaugurated by Saint Pius X and the Second Vatican Council. But what did surprise me was the fact that at this liturgy it was, apart from the choir members, only children who received. Mothers who approached with babes in arm did not receive. Rather, Father dipped his thumb in the chalice and put it in the little one's mouth. Toddlers were fed with the spoon. As one mother tugged vigorously to bring a recalcitrant four-year-old forward the old pastor cajoled sweetly. If I had not been so amazed by the scene, I think I would have found it highly amusing. But the congregation seemed to take it very much in stride.

Our Lord sat down weary after a long day on the road. Many had reached out to him and power went forth from him; he cured every sort of malady. Many comforting and challenging words had been said. There was the usual rabbinical sparring with the scribes. And, as usual, there was the bickering among his own boys: who was to be first, who most important. It was almost unbelievable. And now as he sat enjoying the evening cool with its special scents, looking forward to his well-earned meal, the sound of their officious voices again reached his ears. Some importunate mothers had arrived with their little ones. "Couldn't the Master just lay his hands on them and bless them. It would bring them luck. Then they would grow and prosper." "No! No! No! He has had enough for one day. He has already blessed hundreds, if not thousands. He even raised a

73

little girl to life. Can't you leave him alone for just a little? Give him a little rest! We're in charge! Now, go away!" Jesus was weary, very weary. But this he could not tolerate. His indignation renewed his strength. He raised his voice: *Let the children come to me, and do not hinder them, for to such belongs the kingdom of God.* Soon they were clambering all over him. His weariness was gone. Renewed in their liveliness, basking in their warm trusting affection. *Truly, I say to you, whoever does not receive the kingdom of God like a child shall not enter it.* He hugged them, kissed them, blessed them again and again. Their mothers, very content, dragged them, not so content, away (they wanted to stay and stay). His weariness returned but now with a warm contentment about it, too.

God has a very special love for little ones. The Scriptures make it most evident. Orthodox Christians, holding fast to the catechesis that intimately bonds the three sacraments of initiation, always administer them together; baptism, Chrismation (confirmation), and Eucharist. Hence little ones receive their first Holy Communion at their baptism and are welcomed to the table of the Lord ever after. This was once a universal practice in the Church; it was lost in the West along with the general withdrawal from Eucharistic intimacy. Until the renewal of Saint Pius X in this century, most lay persons approached the altar only once a year and first Communion was delayed until adolescence. The saintly Pontiff knew the heart of Christ and so urged little ones to approach the sacrament, although he did restrict this to children who, in their parents' judgment, were old enough to be able to discern the difference between the sacred bread and regular bread. Actually this discernment probably comes at quite an early age if children are brought regularly to the liturgy and are given some explanation of what they see. An Orthodox priest told me that a child less than one year old will discern the chalice. Seeing it his eyes light up and his mouth opens eagerly. Saint Pius was speaking of a somewhat more conceptual discernment than this which comes only from experience.

Whether the Western Church should continue to hold to her present criterion is being questioned by pastors who see the value of children truly growing up with the things of God, familiar with them as part of the fabric of life. Be that as it may, it would be well to act according to the prescriptions of Saint Pius. Parental freedom in this matter has been largely co-opted by parochial authorities organizing group first communions or dictating when parents can first bring their children to the altar. Parents should lovingly introduce their little ones to Holy Communion as soon as they see they know the special bread is Jesus, to whom they talk in prayer. If the family prays together regularly and the little ones go regularly with the parents to Mass, even three-year-olds in many cases would, I suspect, be able to make this connection. Parents are the judges.

Mother Church is concerned about her little ones. In 1973 Pope Paul VI mandated a *Directory for Masses with Children*. This could be most parish Masses. Indeed, having Masses with only children present is discouraged. It is urged that they be integrated into the full Eucharistic assembly. The directory gives the celebrant the faculties and the responsibility to accommodate the liturgy to the capacity of his young participants. He may adopt or choose alternate prayers and readings. The introductory rite may be modified to retain only one of the elements. Simplicity is encouraged. The readings may be reduced to one, introduced with an explanation. The homily is deemed very important and can be in dialogue form. Another direct appeal to the children before the dismissal is encouraged. The Apostles' Creed may be used.

Soon after Pope Paul's mandate, three new Eucharistic Prayers for Masses with children were approved. They are shorter and simpler than the other prayers, with more acclamations to allow for greater active participation. Sad to say, in most parishes both the use of the faculties for adaptation and the use of these canons have been relegated to occasional "children's Masses." That is certainly not what was intended. They were meant, as the documents say, for Masses *with* children—many parish Masses would qualify. These adaptations and canons do demand more of the celebrant. He has to be creative and cannot just read the texts. The use of them would, I have no doubt, be very beneficial for the adults present, as well as for the children. Children should be more fully incorporated into parochial liturgy. They need to know they belong. Moreover, it will be effective for the adults as well. Have a seven-year-old do a short, simple first reading and every parent in the church will wait expectantly for every single word. Have a little one carry the cruets up the aisle and every eye will be on that offertory procession. As the directory says, "Adults can also benefit spiritually from experiencing the part which the children have within the Christian community."

Any priest who has the heart of Chirst will never celebrate the Eucharist without being very conscious of any children who are present, and, while not neglecting the needs of the parents and elders, will not fail to make provision for the children's eager minds and hearts. The demand to make the celebration relevant to them will challenge him to attain greater clarity and simplicity, and thus improve his overall effectiveness, personal involvement, and commitment. *Let the children come.* The kingdom of heaven is theirs, the heavenly places in which we celebrate, and, since the kingdom is theirs, they can give it to us.

EUCHARISTIC PRAYERS FOR MASS WITH CHILDREN

Prayer I

The Lord be with you.

And also with you.

Lift up your hearts.

We lift them up to the Lord.

Let us give thanks to the Lord our God.

It is right to give him thanks and praise.

God our Father,
you have brought us here together
so that we can give you thanks and praise
for all the wonderful things you have done.

We thank you for all that is beautiful in the world
and for the happiness you have given us.
We praise you for daylight
and for your word which lights up our minds.
We praise you for the earth,
and all the people who live on it,
and for our life which comes from you.

We know that you are good.
You love us and do great things for us.
So we all sing together:

*Holy, holy, holy Lord, God of power and might,
heaven and earth are full of your glory.
Hosanna in the highest.*

Father,
you are always thinking about your people;
you never forget us.
You sent us your Son Jesus,
who gave his life for us
and who came to save us.

He cured sick people;
he cared for those who were poor
and wept with those who were sad.
He forgave sinners
and taught us to forgive each other.
He loved everyone
and showed us how to be kind.
He took children in his arms and blessed them.
So we are glad to sing:

> *Blessed is he who comes in the name of the Lord.*
>   *Hosanna in the highest.*

God our Father,
all over the world your people praise you.
So now we pray with the whole Church:
with John Paul, our pope and our bishop.
In heaven the blessed Virgin Mary,
the apostles and all the saints
always sing your praise.
Now we join with them and with the angels
to adore you as we sing:

> *Holy, holy, holy Lord, God of power and might,*
> *heaven and earth are full of your glory.*
>   *Hosanna in the highest.*
> *Blessed is he who comes in the name of the Lord.*
>   *Hosanna in the highest.*

God our Father,
you are most holy
and we want to show you that we are grateful.

We bring you bread and wine
and ask you to send your Holy Spirit to make these gifts
the body and blood of Jesus your Son.
Then we can offer to you
what you have given to us.

On the night before he died,
Jesus was having supper with his apostles.
He took bread from the table.

He gave you thanks and praise.
Then he broke the bread, gave it to his friends, and said:
Take this, all of you, and eat it:
this is my body which will be given up for you.

When the supper was ended,
Jesus took the cup that was filled with wine.
He thanked you, gave it to his friends, and said:
Take this, all of you, and drink from it:
this is the cup of my blood,
the blood of the new and everlasting covenant.
It will be shed for you and for all
so that sins may be forgiven.
Then he said to them:
do this in memory of me.

We do now what Jesus told us to do.
We remember his death and his resurrection
and we offer you, Father, the bread that gives us life,
and the cup that saves us.
Jesus brings us to you;
welcome us as you welcome him.

Let us proclaim our faith:

> *When we eat this bread and drink this cup,*
> *we proclaim your death, Lord Jesus,*
> *until you come in glory.*

Father,
because you love us,
you invite us to come to your table.
Fill us with the joy of the Holy Spirit
as we receive the body and blood of your Son.

Lord,
you never forget any of your children.
We ask you to take care of those we love,
especially . . . ,
and we pray for those who have died.

Remember everyone who is suffering from pain or sorrow.
Remember Christians everywhere
and all other people in the world.

We are filled with wonder and praise
when we see what you do for us
through Jesus your Son,
and so we sing:

> *Through him,*
> *with him,*
> *in him,*
> *in the unity of the Holy Spirit,*
> *all glory and honor is yours,*
> *almighty Father,*
> *for ever and ever.*
> *Amen.*

Prayer II

The Lord be with you.

> *And also with you.*

Lift up your hearts.

> *We lift them up to the Lord.*

Let us give thanks to the Lord our God.

> *It is right to give him thanks and praise.*

God, our loving Father,
we are glad to give you thanks and praise
because you love us.
With Jesus we sing your praise:

> *Glory to God in the highest.*

Because you love us,
you gave us this great and beautiful world.
With Jesus we sing your praise:

Glory to God in the highest.

Because you love us,
you sent Jesus your Son
to bring us to you
and to gather us around him
as the children of one family.
With Jesus we sing your praise:

Glory to God in the highest.

For such great love
we thank you with the angels and saints
as they praise you and sing:

> *Holy, holy, holy Lord, God of power and might,*
> *heaven and earth are full of your glory.*
> *Hosanna in the highest.*
> *Blessed is he who comes in the name of the Lord.*
> *Hosanna in the highest.*

Blessed be Jesus, whom you sent
to be the friend of children and of the poor.

He came to show us
how we can love you, Father,
by loving one another.
He came to take away sin,
which keeps us from being friends,
and hate, which makes us all unhappy.

He promised to send the Holy Spirit,
to be with us always
so that we can live as your children.

> *Blessed is he who comes in the name of the Lord.*
> *Hosanna in the highest.*

God our Father,
we now ask you
to send your Holy Spirit

to change these gifts of bread and wine
into the body and blood
of Jesus Christ, our Lord.

The night before he died,
Jesus your Son showed us how much you love us.
When he was at supper with his disciples,
he took bread,
and gave you thanks and praise.
Then he broke the bread,
gave it to his friends, and said:
Take this, all of you, and eat it:
this is my body which will be given up for you.

> *Jesus has given his life for us.*

When supper was ended,
Jesus took the cup that was filled with wine.
He thanked you, gave it to his friends, and said:
Take this, all of you, and drink from it:
this is the cup of my blood,
the blood of the new and everlasting covenant.
It will be shed for you and for all
so that sins may be forgiven.

> *Jesus has given his life for us.*

Then he said to them:
do this in memory of me.

And so, loving Father,
we remember that Jesus died and rose again
to save the world.
He put himself into our hands
to be the sacrifice we offer you.

> *We praise you, we bless you, we thank you.*

Lord our God,
listen to our prayer.
Send the Holy Spirit
to all of us who share in this meal.

May this Spirit bring us closer together
in the family of the Church,
with John Paul, our pope,
our bishop,
all other bishops,
and all who serve your people.

We praise you, we bless you, we thank you.

Remember, Father, our families and friends...,
and all those we do not love as we should.
Remember those who have died....
Bring them home to you
to be with you for ever.

We praise you, we bless you, we thank you.

Gather us all together into your kingdom.
There we shall be happy for ever
with the Virgin Mary, Mother of God and our mother.
There all the friends
of Jesus the Lord
will sing a song of joy.

We praise you, we bless you, we thank you.

Through him,
with him,
in him,
in the unity of the Holy Spirit,
all glory and honor is yours,
almighty Father,
for ever and ever.

Amen.

Prayer III

The Lord be with you.

And also with you.

Lift up your hearts.

> *We lift them up to the Lord.*

Let us give thanks to the Lord our God.

> *It is right to give him thanks and praise.*

We thank you,
God our Father.

You made us to live for you and for each other.
We can see and speak to one another,
and become friends,
and share our joys and sorrows.

And so, Father, we gladly thank you
with every one who believes in you;
with the saints and the angels,
we rejoice and praise you, saying:

> *Holy, holy, holy Lord, God of power and might,*
> *heaven and earth are full of your glory.*
> > *Hosanna in the highest.*
> *Blessed is he who comes in the name of the Lord.*
> > *Hosanna in the highest.*

Yes, Lord, you are holy;
you are kind to us and to all men.
For this we thank you.
We thank you above all for your Son, Jesus Christ.

You sent him into this world
because people had turned away from you
and no longer loved each other.
He opened our eyes and our hearts
to understand that we are brothers and sisters
and that you are Father of us all.

He now brings us together to one table
and asks us to do what he did.

Father,
we ask you to bless these gifts of bread and wine
and make them holy.
Change them for us into the body and blood of
   Jesus Christ, your Son.

On the night before he died for us,
he had supper for the last time with his disciples.
He took bread
and gave you thanks.
He broke the bread
and gave it to his friends, saying:
Take this, all of you, and eat it:
this is my body which will be given up for you.

In the same way he took a cup of wine.
He gave you thanks
and handed the cup to his disciples, saying:
Take this, all of you, and drink from it:
this is the cup of my blood,
the blood of the new and everlasting covenant.
It will be shed for you and for all
so that sins may be forgiven.
Then he said to them:
do this in memory of me.

God our Father,
we remember with joy
all that Jesus did to save us.
In this holy sacrifice,
which he gave as a gift to his Church,
we remember his death and resurrection.

Father in heaven,
accept us together with your beloved Son.
He willingly died for us,
but you raised him to life again.
We thank you and say:

   Glory to God in the highest.

Jesus now lives with you in glory,
but he is also here on earth, among us.
We thank you and say:

Glory to God in the highest.

One day he will come in glory
and in his kingdom
there will be no more suffering,
no more tears, no more sadness.
We thank you and say:

Glory to God in the highest.

Father in heaven,
you have called us
to receive the body and blood of Christ at this table
and to be filled with the joy of the Holy Spirit.
Through this sacred meal
give us strength to please you more and more.

Lord, our God,
remember John Paul, our pope,
our bishop, and all other bishops.

Help all who follow Jesus
to work for peace
and to bring happiness to others.

Bring us all at last
together with Mary, the Mother of God,
and all the saints,
to live with you
and to be one with Christ in heaven.

Through him,
with him,
in him,
in the unity of the Holy Spirit,
all glory and honor is yours,
almighty Father,
for ever and ever.

Amen.

WE WANT MORE

✤ ✤ ✤

Undoubtedly one of the most difficult Masses a priest has to preside at is the funeral Mass of his mother. Even just thinking of it now my eyes begin to burn with tears.

There has been a beautiful custom in the Catholic community. On ordination day the hands of the new priest are anointed with oil. Then they are wrapped with a special cloth. My sister-in-law had prepared mine, embroidering on it in blue my motto: "For me to live is Christ." When the hands are unbound, after the priest has received the symbols of his new ministry, the cloth is used to wipe off the excess oil. Then it is carefully rolled up and given to the mother of the priest. It will next be seen in her hands as she lays in her coffin, proclaiming to all that she is the mother of a priest.

As I looked down at those hands and that symbol I realized that while my priesthood was brought to sacramental fullness and my ministry integrated into the Church when Cardinal Wright laid his hands on my head, it had begun in the womb of this woman. The ministerial priesthood is grounded in and comes out of the priesthood of the faithful, especially the faith of mothers. If we have a shortage of priests today we need to look to the homes. Do mothers today want to nurture their children to serve the people of God? The home is the *only* source of priests. When mothers consider it a privilege and joy to mother priests we will have priests. If parochial and other groups feel the lack of priests—and they will more and more unless there is a sudden change—they need first look to themselves and their role to nurture persons for ministry.

Some priests of more powerful faith, or perhaps of calmer temperament, can handle well the funeral liturgy for their mother. It does have its own most special joy and cause for celebration. But most of us are of more fragile human fabric. I was happy to have a lifelong friend at my side, a priest-classmate who knew Mom well. He did a beautiful job on the homily. I will be ever grateful to him for that. But it was a great consolation for me, as the celebrant, when I came to the place in the third Eucharistic Prayer where I could pray very specifically for my mother

86

and place our present sorrow firmly in the context of the final fullness we would share:

> Remember Helene, my mother. In baptism she died with Christ; may she also share his resurrection, when Christ will raise our mortal bodies and make them like his own in glory. Welcome into your kingdom our departed brothers and sisters, and all who have left this world in your friendship. There we hope to share in your glory, when every tear will be wiped away. On that day we shall see you, our God, as you are. We shall become like you and praise you forever through Christ our Lord, from whom all good things come.

The Mass is very much at the heart of Christian life as we Catholics experience it. Some have even felt we have made too much of the Mass. It has supplanted almost every other form of communal worship. The Hours of the Liturgy are rarely celebrated in parishes although they are again finding a place in the lives of religious and in other communities. Most devotions have been absorbed into the Mass. We seek to make the Mass a part of all our significant events: We have Masses for baptisms, first Communions, confirmations, graduations, weddings, ordinations, professions, funerals, and anniversaries of all sorts. We have Masses for Thanksgiving, Independence Day, Election Day, and Labor Day. The renewed sacramentary gives us appropriate prayers for most of these and special prefaces for the more important ones.

It is good and right that the Mass should be tightly woven into the fabric of our lives. It is the source of our life as Christians; all the empowering we receive for each of the significant events in our lives, and for the daily life between them, comes from and through the Mass. The Mass expresses, as only infinite love can, the fullness that is at the heart of our lives. It is good when these special events can be woven into the fabric of the Mass. The option given us in the Third Eucharistic Prayer to bring the death of a loved one with all our feeling and faith-filled hope right into the great prayer is very consoling and empowering.

We want more of this.

Pope Paul VI, that great pastor, knew this. When in 1974 he proclaimed a Holy Year of Reconciliation for the following year he also decreed that there should be special Eucharistic Prayers of Reconciliation, so that the year and its meaning could find a most intimate place in the life of the Christian community. These Eucharistic Prayers remain in use, helping us in communal celebrations of the sacrament of reconciliation, and helping us to enter into the spirit of conversion during the holy season of Lent and at other times. Like the Eucharistic Prayers for Masses with children, these prayers are marked by simplicity and clarity. There are marked by a proclamation of reconciliation, one that reminds us that we must be reconciled not only with God but with one another: *If, coming to the altar, you remember your brother or sister has something against you, leave your gift at the altar and go, first be reconciled with your brother or sister and then come and offer your sacrifice.* "Your Spirit changes our hearts: enemies begin to speak to one another, those who were estranged join hands in friendship and nations seek the way of peace together." "Keep us all in communion of mind and heart."

In the early Church, the bishop or priest who presided at the Eucharist had the responsibility of formulating the anaphora. Thus he was able to adapt it to the immediate celebration. The introduction into our liturgy in recent years of a great number of variable parts (most notably prefaces, but also the eight additional canons) allows the principal celebrant to make a selection that suits the occasion. We can hope, though, that as liturgical education and experience grow, the freedom and responsibility of the celebrant will increase until he has all the space he needs to adapt each Eucharistic celebration to the particular gathering.

Such freedom has its dangers, of course, and therefore its responsibility. There is the danger of centering the liturgy too much on everyday life, of reducing it to a celebration of the human—social, political, even revolutionary. The Eucharist and human life should form one fabric, but in the weaving the mystery should not be reduced. On the contrary, human life should be lifted up and transformed, filled with a faith and a hope that points to something beyond, to divinization. Even with the freedom that the priest and the people today can bring into their celebration, care should always be taken not to obscure the true nature and essential elements of the Eucharist. It must always be clear that it is first and foremost a *memoria* of Christ's paschal mystery. All his other mysteries, all the victories of Mary and the saints, all the events of our lives are celebrated in the light of this central event. It is this that gives us cause to celebrate anything and everything: *If Christ be not risen from the dead then our faith is in vain and we are the most foolish of men.* This *memoria* involves a sacrifice, a making present of Christ in sacrifice, and a union of our sacrifice through and with his—a giving to God to bring about union with him. And in the Mass this is always fulfilled in a sacrificial meal. Neither the sacrifice of Christ nor our sacrifice—the sacrifice of the Church —should be lost sight of. Neither should the celebration of the sacrifice obscure the meal itself (as was so much the case in times when Communion was a rarity) nor the celebration of the meal obscure the sacrifice (a greater danger in our time, especially in informal and home Eucharists).

One of the things that is most evident in this is the need for the priest to be well prepared to lead the Eucharist. He must have not only a good understanding of the Mass and all its theological elements, along with a real sense of the gathering and where it is in the pilgrimage of salvation, but depth of spirituality—openness and sensitivity to the Spirit so as to be instinctively guided by him—that can integrate and harmonize these elements. (I will say more about this in the next chapter.)

For now my plea is that we will have the courage to continue to pursue liturgical renewal. In many places discontent and apathy are due to the fact that what we have already received by way of new liturgical instruction, direction, law, and texts has not been effectively brought into living experience. This may be largely the fault of the pastoral leadership. But the people cannot be fully excused. With them remains the responsibility of calling the pastors forth, demanding more, and supporting the effort. But even in communities where the renewal has been fully implemented there is dissatisfaction. There is in such communities an ever growing desire to bring life and liturgy into greater interpenetration and oneness.

Responsible creativity must be constantly encouraged. The priest and the people need to have the space and the responsibility to celebrate the paschal mystery as they are now experiencing and living it as a community, never as a community in isolation, but in the Church as a part of the whole Christ. Thus, parameters are established both by the nature of the paschal mystery and its liturgical Eucharistic celebration and by the nature of the community as of the Church. Liturgical norms should make these clear and at the same time make clear how they flow from the very nature of reality. Within these parameters the greatest possible freedom should prevail so that the community can properly and responsibly celebrate its own immediate experience of these realities. The principle laid down by the first Council of Jerusalem should always prevail: "It is the decision of the Holy Spirit, and ours too, not to lay on you any burden beyond that which is strictly necessary" (Acts 15:28). Certainly, more instruction, a continued sharing of both new texts and old ones, and a clarification and development of roles and ministries are desirable—all in service of a greater freedom and responsibility for the particular gathering to celebrate the Mass as its own in Christ in the Church.

EUCHARISTIC PRAYERS
FOR MASSES OF RECONCILIATION

Prayer I

The Lord be with you.

And also with you.

Lift up your hearts.

We lift them up to the Lord.

Let us give thanks to the Lord our God.

It is right to give him thanks and praise.

Father, all-powerful and ever-living God,
we do well always and everywhere to give you thanks
    and praise.
You never cease to call us
to a new and more abundant life.

God of love and mercy,
you are always ready to forgive;
we are sinners,
and you invite us
to trust in your mercy.

Time and time again
we broke your covenant,
but you did not abandon us.
Instead, through your Son, Jesus our Lord,
you bound yourself even more closely to the human family
by a bond that can never be broken.

Now is the time
for your people to turn back to you
and to be renewed in Christ your Son,
a time of grace and reconciliation.

You invite us
to serve the family of mankind
by opening our hearts
to the fullness of your Holy Spirit.

In wonder and gratitude,
we join our voices with the choirs of heaven
to proclaim the power of your love
and to sing of our salvation in Christ:

Holy, holy, holy Lord, God of power and might,
heaven and earth are full of your glory.
  Hosanna in the highest.
Blessed is he who comes in the name of the Lord.
  Hosanna in the highest.

Father,
from the beginning of time
you have always done what is good for us
so that we may be holy as you are holy.

Look with kindness on your people
gathered here before you:
send forth the power of your Spirit
so that these gifts may become for us
the body and blood of your beloved Son, Jesus the Christ,
in whom we have become your sons and daughters.

When we were lost
and could not find the way to you,
you loved us more than ever:
Jesus, your Son, innocent and without sin,
gave himself into our hands
and was nailed to a cross.
Yet before he stretched out his arms between
    heaven and earth
in the everlasting sign of your covenant,
he desired to celebrate the Paschal feast
in the company of his disciples.

While they were at supper,
he took bread and gave you thanks and praise.
He broke the bread, gave it to his disciples, and said:
Take this, all of you, and eat it:
this is my body which will be given up for you.
At the end of the meal,
knowing that he was to reconcile all things in himself
by the blood of his cross,
he took the cup, filled with wine.
Again he gave you thanks, handed the cup to his
    friends, and said:
Take this, all of you, and drink from it:

this is the cup of my blood,
the blood of the new and everlasting covenant.
It will be shed for you and for all
so that sins may be forgiven.
Do this in memory of me.

Let us proclaim the mystery of faith:

> *Dying you destroyed our death,*
> *rising you restored our life.*
> *Lord Jesus, come in glory.*

We do this in memory of Jesus Christ,
our Passover and our lasting peace.
We celebrate his death and resurrection
and look for the coming of that day
when he will return to give us the fullness of joy.
Therefore we offer you, God ever faithful and true,
the sacrifice which restores man to your friendship.

Father,
look with love
on those you have called
to share in the one sacrifice of Christ.
By the power of your Holy Spirit
make them one body,
healed of all division.

Keep us all
in communion of mind and heart
with John Paul, our pope, and our bishop.
Help us to work together
for the coming of your kingdom,
until at last we stand in your presence
to share the life of the saints,
in the company of the Virgin Mary and the apostles,
and of our departed brothers and sisters
whom we commend to your mercy.

Then, freed from every shadow of death,
we shall take our place in the new creation
and give you thanks
with Christ, our risen Lord.

Through him,
with him,
in him,
in the unity of the Holy Spirit,
all glory and honor is yours,
almighty Father,
for ever and ever.

Amen.

Prayer II

The Lord be with you.

And also with you.

Lift up your hearts.

We lift them up to the Lord.

Let us give thanks to the Lord our God.

It is right to give him thanks and praise.

Father, all-powerful and ever-living God,
we praise and thank you through Jesus Christ our Lord
for your presence and action in the world.

In the midst of conflict and division,
we know it is you
who turn our minds to thoughts of peace.
Your Spirit changes our hearts:
enemies begin to speak to one another,
those who were estranged join hands in friendship,
and nations seek the way of peace together.

Your Spirit is at work
when understanding puts an end to strife,
when hatred is quenched by mercy,
and vengeance gives way to forgiveness.

For this we should never cease
to thank and praise you.
We join with all the choirs of heaven
as they sing for ever to your glory:

> *Holy, holy, holy Lord, God of power and might.*
> *Heaven and earth are full of your glory.*
> > *Hosanna in the highest.*
> *Blessed is he who comes in the name of the Lord.*
> > *Hosanna in the highest.*

God of power and might,
we praise you through your Son, Jesus Christ,
who comes in your name.
He is the Word that brings salvation.
He is the hand you stretch out to sinners.
He is the way that leads to your peace.

God our Father,
we had wandered far from you,
but through your Son you have brought us back.
You gave him up to death
so that we might turn again to you
and find our way to one another.

Therefore we celebrate the reconciliation
Christ has gained for us.
We ask you to sanctify these gifts
by the power of your Spirit,
as we now fulfill your Son's command.

While he was at supper
on the night before he died for us,
he took bread in his hands,
and gave you thanks and praise.
He broke the bread,
gave it to his disciples, and said:
Take this, all of you, and eat it:
this is my body which will be given up for you.
At the end of the meal he took the cup.
Again he praised you for your goodness,
gave the cup to his disciples, and said:

Take this, all of you, and drink from it:
this is the cup of my blood,
the blood of the new and everlasting covenant.
It will be shed for you and for all
so that sins may be forgiven.
Do this is memory of me.

Let us proclaim the mystery of faith:

Lord, by your cross and resurrection
you have set us free.
You are the Savior of the world.

Lord our God,
your Son has entrusted to us
this pledge of his love.
We celebrate the memory of his death and resurrection
and bring you the gift you have given us,
the sacrifice of reconciliation.
Therefore, we ask you, Father,
to accept us, together with your Son.

Fill us with his Spirit
through our sharing in this meal.
May he take away all that divides us.

May this Spirit keep us always in communion
with John Paul, our pope, our bishop,
with all the bishops and all your people.
Father, make your Church throughout the world
a sign of unity and an instrument of your peace.

You have gathered us here
around the table of your Son,
in fellowship with the Virgin Mary, Mother of God,
    and all the saints.

In that new world where the fullness of your peace
    will be revealed,
gather people of every race, language, and way of life
to share in the one eternal banquet
with Jesus Christ the Lord.

Through him,
with him,
in him,
in the unity of the Holy Spirit,
all glory and honor is yours,
almighty Father,
for ever and ever.

   Amen.

A WORD TO THE PRESIDENT

The Mass is at the very heart of our life. It should be. We are called priests because we offer sacrifice—the sacrifice of the Mass. We belong to a priestly people. The Christian has been baptized into Christ, made a partaker of his priesthood. Our priesthood is a ministerial priesthood because it ministers to the priesthood of all the faithful. Fulfilling our role as president of the people gathered, exercising our priesthood, we make it possible for them to exercise their priesthood here and now in a fully sacramental way. The priesthood is at the heart of our ministry; it is its culmination. It is not surprising then that in the Mass we find our greatest joy and source of strength, and also a source of much frustration. The causes of our frustration are various; they depend in part on our expectations.

Older priests can recall the Mass as being the place of fullest and most intimate communion with the Lord, intimacy that empowered the rest of their ministry. The Latin text had become completely familiar. It was pregnant with the devotion of years—the first fervor of the newly ordained, the many practice Masses, the first Mass, the many significant Masses that followed: births and deaths, marriages and ordinations, personal trials and celebrations. The one Latin text flowed quietly along, a powerful background for a very personal encounter with the Lord. The gathered community caused little "distraction." Even as we turned to greet them, the rubrics directed we keep our eyes cast down lest we lose our interior recollection. We had to look at the people only during the homily—which was reserved for Sundays and special occasions—and at the moment of Communion, when our eyes were still more on the Host than on the recipients. We kept our back to the people and our eyes to the Lord.

Now, the people are ever before us; we are expected to be constantly aware of them. Even the anaphora is referred to as a "proclamation."

As a monk whose calling is an option to go apart and enjoy the freedom to be to God alone, I can indeed understand the sense of loss and frustration many older priests experience. But I know, too, that even in the solitary Mass in the monastic cell, if the priest is alive to reality, he is keenly aware that he is not alone with the Alone: he stands there with Christ before the Father in communion with every man, woman, and child on earth. The new format of the Eucharist, casting the president into the midst of the priestly people, constantly aware of them and one with them, corresponds visibly and sacramentally to this reality.

The priest-mediator does need his time to be alone with the Alone. Some element of this should probably be woven into the Eucharistic celebration. In the Eastern rite there is a moment when the veil is drawn, allowing the priest to pray in silence, in a very personal way, before receiving his Lord. But the Mass as a whole is not the time for this solitary, personal, and empowering communion. The priest needs to go into his room and close the door and pray to his Father in secret, as our Master has told us. Then, coming to the altar, he will experience a satisfying level of communion with the Lord, even in the midst of the people.

Younger priests who have never experienced the Latin liturgy with the priest turning his back to the people do not come to the Eucharist with the same expectations, nor experience the same frustrations. For them the Eucharist is a place of encounter, of communion. They are very conscious that they stand as the priestly leader of these people, to bring God's Word and gift to them now, where they are, and to give voice to their immediate prayer to God. These priests' frustration arises more from being restricted by rubrics and by texts that do not seem to be flexible enough to meet the real needs of the assembly here and now.

I have already stated my conviction that the liturgical renewal should continue to move toward giving the president greater freedom and responsibility in leading the Eucharistic assembly in expressing itself in the Church. I would like to say two other things here.

First, I think it is important that the priest be sure that he fully uses the responsible freedom that the present liturgical provisions give him. In my own experience, I have found few priests who do fully exercise their responsibility to adapt the present liturgy to the particular celebration. A careful study of the Apostolic Constitution of Paul VI, the General Instruction and the Foreword of the Sacramentary, and other relevant documents is called for. Let me just quote a few sentences:

> Without a thorough knowledge of the general instruction it is impossible for the priest to understand the conciliar reform and to take the principal role in planning the celebration with the other ministers and all who have special responsibility for it. (Foreword)

Some elements of the liturgy are underlined in a renewed way:

a homily, as a living explanation of the word, increases its effectiveness and is an integral part of the service. (General Instruction, no. 9)

Silence should be observed at designated times as a part of the celebration. Its character will depend on the time it occurs in the particular celebration. At the penitential rite and again after the invitation to pray, each one should become recollected; at the conclusion of a reading or the homily, each one meditates briefly on what he has heard; after Communion he praises God in his heart and prays. (ibid., no. 23)

The Foreword adds:

Just as there should be no celebration without song, so too there should be no celebration without periods for silent prayer and reflection.

The awesome fullness of the president's role is spelled out:

Within the community of the faithful a presbyter also possesses the power of orders to offer sacrifice as the Person of Christ. He presides over the assembly and leads its prayer, proclaims the message of salvation, leads the people in offering sacrifice through Christ in the Spirit to the Father, gives them the Bread of Eternal Life and shares it with them. At the Eucharist he should serve God and the people with dignity and humility. By his actions and by his proclamation of the word he should impress upon the faithful the living presence of Christ. (General Instruction, no. 13)

The practical effectiveness of a celebration depends in great measure on choosing readings, prayers and songs which correspond to the needs, spiritual preparation, and attitude of the participants. . . . In planning the celebration the priest should consider the spiritual good of the assembly rather than his own desires. The choice of texts is to be made in consultation with the minister and those who have a function in the celebration, including the faithful, for the parts which belong to them. (ibid., no. 313)

. . . the celebration takes into account the nature and circumstances of each assembly and is planned to bring about conscious, active, and full participation of the people, motivated by faith, hope and charity. (ibid., no.3)

In addition to the selection of appropriate texts, a truly living and communal celebration requires the president and all other ministers to examine carefully different forms of verbal communication with the congregation. This refers to the readings, homily, admonition, introduction, and similar parts. (Foreword)

Texts translated from another language are clearly not sufficient for the celebration of a fully renewed liturgy. The creation of new texts will be necessary. But translation of texts transmitted through the tradition of the Church is the best school and discipline for the creation of new texts, in that any new forms adopted should in some way grow organically from forms already in existence. (Letter, Congregation for Divine Worship, April 27, 1977)

The formula must become the genuine prayer of the congregation, and in it each of its members should be able to find the expression of himself. (Instruction of the Consilium for Implementation of the Constitution on the Liturgy, no. 20)

The prayers (opening prayer, prayer over the gifts, prayer after Communion, and the prayer over the people) from the ancient Roman tradition are succinct and abstract. In translation they may need to be rendered somewhat more fully while conserving the original ideas. This can be done by moderately amplifying them, or, if necessary, paraphrasing expressions in order to concretize them for the celebration and needs of today. In every case, pompous and superfluous language should be avoided. (ibid., no. 34)

If the priest uses his own words, the invitatory can be more concrete and effective. (Letter, Congregation for Divine Worship, April 27, 1977)

By their nature these brief admonitions do not require that everyone use them in the form in which they appear in the missal. Provision can be made in certain cases that they may be adapted to some degree to the varying circumstances of the community. (Foreword)

Insight and a certain freedom should go into the composition of these intercessions. . . . (ibid.)

In addition, the individual Mass formularies for Sundays in the principal seasons and on other occasions give a suggested example so that the pattern may become clear. (ibid.)

He may use a different but similar formula. (ibid.)

We sense here, in reading through the many pages of introduction in the Sacramentary and the various documents, an effort in the renewal to return to the freedom and responsibility of the early Church, as prescribed in the *Apostolic Tradition* of Hippolytus:

The bishop shall give thanks according to what we have given. It is not at all necessary for him to say the same words, as though reciting them from memory, when he gives thanks to God. Let each pray according to his gift. If he has the gift of praying at length and with solemnity, that is a good thing. But if anyone prays briefly, there should be no objection. What matters is that his prayer should be orthodox.

This flexibility is carried over into some of the rubrics of the Missal of Paul VI, where we read such directions as:

> . . . he invites them to pray, using these or similar words.

> He may use these or similar words.

> At the discretion of the priest, other words which seem more suitable under the circumstances . . . may be used. This also applies to parallel instances in the liturgy.

I believe if the president fully employs all the opportunities offered by the present liturgical texts to adapt the liturgy and its expression to the present gathering he will have a service very attuned to the people.

The opening rite is most important. It is a movement of conversion, but it need not always center on sin. Usually those who have gathered have already turned from sin. It is rather a question of a fuller conversion through a participation in the mystery to be celebrated. Joy and thanksgiving are an implicit rejection of the gloominess and bondage of sin. The opening rite is an entrance into a new state of being, a freedom from sin, surely, but a freedom to God and all the fullness of Christian community. The president, sensing the power of the mystery to be celebrated and perceiving where the gathered people are on their journey, calls them forth to take that next step in faithfulness.

In the English missal for the Sundays and major feasts we find alternate opening prayers. These have been prepared by my confrere Father Robert Morehouse, O.C.S.O. He is presently preparing alternate texts for the ferial days. These texts are meant to assist the president in formulating the apt prayer for the assembly here and now. So, too, for other prayers at the offering of the gifts and at Communion. The president is to gather up and express the prayer of the people assembled.

The president is free to introduce the readings and every other important part of the liturgy in any way that will help the assembly to benefit by it. His homily is his major word to them, but the other brief introductions may require as much prayerful preparation and be very effective in their conciseness. His opening into the anaphora and then into the Communion service should help the whole congregation to move together in mind and heart. His words at the dismissal should gather up the fullness of the experience and send the people forth empowered.

Up to this point we have spoken primarily of the content of the liturgy and its expression. But while the content is important (and the liturgical renewal needed and still needs to do much in this regard), true renewal will never be effected by a change in content alone—some have gone to almost incredible lengths, and yet have not produced the results for which they labored. There needs to be a shift in *context*.

Recently, I was invited to preside at Sunday Mass in a local parish. At the end of the Mass I received a standing ovation. The pastor remarked: "That never happened before in this parish!" As I shared this with other priests, inevitably they asked, "What did you do?" expecting to hear of some creative form of introduction, some special rites, some innovations. In fact, however, I simply adhered to all the rubrics and used the texts given in the Sacramentary for that Sunday. There was no change in content in my Mass—only a shift in context.

This is where I come to my second point. It is not easy to define exactly what I mean by context. It is the space we come out of, a space that creates space for others. It is opening space in our own lives to let the deep creative forces within us, the divine creative energies, flow forth and call forth the deeper aspirations and responses of those with whom we share. In liturgy, it is coming forth from the reality that we are Christ's priestly people with all the power and love of his priesthood flowing through us. Of its nature, context incarnates solidarity. There are no longer priest and people—so often experienced in apartness—but one Christed people to the Father in fulfillment.

How do we come to this space where we create context? We go into our room and close the door and pray with our Father in secret. We go to the center, to the cell within, and abide at the source of our being. We die in some way to self, to the limitations of our thoughts and concepts, feelings and emotions, opening the space for the common sense of a divinized people to flow. We make space for the Spirit of God, for *we do not know how to pray as we ought*.

Let us resort for a moment to some scholastic theology. The scholastics distinguished the natural virtues, the supernatural virtues, and the gifts of the Holy Spirit. By natural virtues we make judgments and act in the light of reason. By supernatural virtues we make judgments and act in the light of the infused virtues, especially faith, hope, and charity. By the gifts of the Holy Spirit we make judgments and act by the instinct of the Holy Spirit dwelling in us. At baptism we received these gifts, these dispositions to allow the Spirit to guide us. But God profoundly respects our freedom. He will not force us to attend to this guidance and follow it. We can follow our own lights as long as we wish. What we learn in deep prayer is how to listen to the Spirit and act according to his instinct. The gift of knowledge enables us to know in that deep experiential way, to sense God in everyone and everything; to approach all with an instinctive reverence. Understanding enables us to "stand under," to be in touch with what is under the surface, what lies within. Wisdom brings all this to fullness and completion in joy. Under the instinct of the Spirit we sense the deepest meanings of the liturgy we are celebrating, where the gathering is in its spiritual journey and aspiration, and how these flow together so that the liturgy really meets the deeper aspirations of the people (even when they themselves are not at first consciously aware of them) and leads them forth to a new sense of fulfillment. All this happens beyond the level of rational analysis, but in the space or context that has been created by the president and entered into by the assembly.

There is then a very real interconnection between the time the priest spends in his room or in the cell of his heart in centering or contemplative prayer and his presiding successfully at the liturgical assembly. When he is a truly centered man the moments of silence in the liturgy will be powerfully creating a context that will embrace the whole community and transform the content. The content remains important. It must be well prepared. It needs to be constantly renewed. But, of itself, it will remain dead—at best, good theater—if it does not find its place in a life-giving context.

The priest who comes out of the context of a pure heart through which the creative divine Spirit can freely flow will not only use the liturgical texts and rites creatively—he will create a living, celebrating community, a community in touch with its own magnificence.

ONE WITH THE FATHER

❊ ❊ ❊

As I passed through gate after gate of the hundred-acre Sri Ranga Temple and saw the long rows of stalls with temple offerings, the Hall of a Thousand Pillars, and the closely guarded inner courts reserved to Hindu men, I felt I was for the first time really in touch with what the great Jerusalem Temple was like in the days of Jesus and long before. Even today as one looks across from Olivet to the Beautiful Gate, imposing even though walled-up and stripped bare, or leans in prayer against one of the mammoth stones of the Wailing Wall, or ascends to the Lions' Gate (called by Christians Saint Stephen's), the remains of the third Temple are awe-inspiring.

Eleachem drove his fine young bullock up the hill ahead of him. A prize yearling sheep lay securely over his shoulder. Soon the animals' blood would flow out around the immense smoking altar, a sign of life-rendering homage to the life-giving One. Their fat and some of their choice parts would be burned. The priests would take other parts. Then Eleachem would gather his large family around him in the outer court and give each his or her portion. It would be a communion, a sacrificial meal.

Sacrifice means not only gift to God, homage, thanksgiving. It also means union with him. Animals were given over to him in homage and thanksgiving for all he had given, the first fruits of herd and flocks. And he by the convenant rituals he established so long ago returned parts to the offerers for a meal celebrating their union with him.

The sacrifice of the New Covenant has again been offered, or, more correctly, it has again been made present in its one offering and we have been able to be again incorporated as co-offerers, priests by baptism, one with the great Priest, the Victim. And now we prepare for the meal of union, communion, with God our Father and with each other, all in his Son. On the night before he died, when the sacrifice was first offered in a ritual meal he lifted his eyes and said:

> I do not pray for these only, but also for those who believe in me through

their word, that they may all be one, even as you, Father, are in me and
I am in you that they also may be one in us. (John 17: 20–21)

The whole emphasis now is on unity and on that fruit of unity, peace.

The great prayer, the anaphora, had been to the Father; the priest's prayer, Christ's prayer, but our prayer, too, because he is our Mediator: *through him*, who is infinitely above us, true God one with the Father; *with him*, beside us, he who became truly one with us in our humanity and calls us no longer servants but friends; *in him*, who has made us one body, he the new Head, one *in the unity of the Holy Spirit*. Thus we can offer the Father *all honor and glory*, the honor and glory due him, infinite honor and glory, for we are one with the divine Son, and his very love is ours. And so we complete the great prayer: *Amen, Amen, Amen.* We endorse it; we make it our very own.

And knowing our solidarity, taught by the Son himself, we now dare to say: *Our Father.* The priest might well take a moment here, awed by the consummation of the great prayer. He must shift directions, be the mediator. He had been with Christ, all to the Father. Now he turns to the other party of the mediation, to us, and invites us to give voice ourselves to this prayer to the Father, for we have truly been reconciled and made most dear children in Christ.

The "Our Father" is not just a formula of prayer. It is a whole school of prayer. One day, an old nun asked Saint Teresa of Avila, "Mother, how can I become a contemplative?" "Say the 'Our Father,' Sister," was the reply, "but take an hour to say it." Only if we do quietly spend time with this great prayer on our own—"Go into your room, close your door, and pray to your Father in secret"—will we ever come to be able to pray it as we ought according to the exhortation of the celebrant. Let us just take a very few minutes to reflect on it here.

The first compelling realization is that we do pray together to *Our* Father. We are truly offspring, one with the Son, one with each other. Rightly do we extol him, rightly do we worship him: *Hallowed be thy name. Thy kingdom come. Thy will be done.* Then again comes the shift from God the Father in heaven to the fabric of this world and we the community of worshiping offspring; the shift from heaven, where everything is indeed done his way, to the unruly earth, where we struggle to do things his way, knowing in our better moments that this is the way to unity and peace and all happiness. *Thy will be done on earth as it is in heaven.*

Give us this day our daily bread. Our Father is very practical and concrete. Jesus assured us: "Your Father knows what you need." Before all else we need bread—food—to live. (A wealthy Catholic underwent a conversion experience. His life turned around to be a complete response to God. "Whatever you do to these the least of mine, you do to me." He founded Food for the Poor and has distributed thousands of cards that say: "To the poor, God comes in the form of bread.") First, we must live. We must have bread to eat. But we do not live by bread alone. We need, we ask for, spiritual food, and at this moment, above all, for the bread of heaven, the Eucharist, the true bread of life.

We go on to pray about all the things that can and do separate us, that hinder our unity and make us unworthy of Communion. Saint Augustine said that "The 'Our Father' is like washing our face before we go to the altar." In the Byzantine rite, as the time of Communion approaches the veil is drawn and the celebrant chants: "Holy Things to the holy." We ask that sin, temptation, and evil be taken away. But there is a rider here. Jesus had said, "Blessed are the merciful for they shall obtain mercy." And he taught us to pray in a rather frightening way: *Forgive us as we forgive.* The temptation to omit the second part can be great. We know how unforgiving we are at times. But Augustine assures us that such an omission will do us no good. God knows the prayer he taught. He operates by no other rules. We are moving toward Communion, but we cannot have communion without union. Forgiveness is essential. It is time to let go, not yield to the temptation to hold back in any way, to accept and embrace the freedom to be able to embrace each and every brother and sister in the shared filiation of God's children. Some have found the kiss of peace a difficulty—the root of the difficulty may lie right here. Our Lord has said: "If your brother has anything against you, leave your gift at the altar; go, first be reconciled with him, and then come." It is ridiculous to do anything else, to seek communion with our Lord in direct contradiction to what he says. It won't work. If, at this moment, we cannot go physically to our offended brother or sister, then let us go in spirit. That will be enough for now. If he or she is in the gathering with us then at the kiss of peace we might seek him out and truly make peace.

The priest expands our prayer—freedom, even freedom from anxiety— so that with joyful hope we can expect our Lord in communion. We pray most confidently because his is the kingdom (everything and everyone is within his domain) and the power (he can bring about all for which we pray) and the glory—he will do it, for his glory and ours. Some Catholics have thought that the insertion of this doxology into the Mass is taking something over from Protestant worship. It is and it isn't. Our Protestant brothers and sisters have largely kept it in their worship services, but it has a long, long history, going back to the first days of Christianity, long before there ever was a Protestant church. It was, in fact, used in the Mass in England before the Reformation. It is part of our common heritage.

The celebrant, our mediator, now takes us back to the upper room, and he speaks very directly and frankly to Jesus:

> Lord Jesus Christ, you said to your apostles: I leave you peace, my peace I give you. Look not on our sins, but on the faith of your Church, and grant us the peace and unity of your kingdom.

Communion without union is impossible. Union without peace is impossible. And so our priest prays: *grant us peace*; and confident that his prayer is heard, he greets us: *The peace of the Lord be with you always.* And he bids us to greet each other.

Perhaps no element of renewal in the celebration of the Eucharist has been so challenging. Touching another means belonging, acceptance, connectedness. We have to break out of our isolation and take responsibilty—be responsible, "able to respond." When we really feel for someone we have no difficulty in touching. We want to embrace; we want to kiss. In the early Church and for many centuries, Christians did indeed kiss each other at the "kiss of peace." Men and women were usually on opposite sides of the assembly (a vestige of Jewish practice), but Saint Paul had insisted that in Christ there was neither male nor female—we are all one in Christ. Reaching out to each other, the members of the body of Christ come together before we together in Communion touch our Head and he touches us most intimately, confirming our oneness.

We should, of course, be mindful at this point of the customs of the place and the situation in which we find ourselves. At charismatic meetings, in monastic communities, in small groups, we might hug each one intimately and even kiss each other. This may be common enough at some parish Masses, also in Latin countries or communities. If, however, the custom in our community is to shake hands, let us do it with meaning, creating a relationship by full presence. If there had been a good, open, warm coming together at the beginning of the gathering, this will happen quite spontaneously. But if this was not the case, let us make the effort now. Look into your brother's eyes, your sister's eyes, smile, take time truly to communicate; use two hands. Be there. Better to be with a few in true communion than superficially jab at all around. We do not want to create or to convey a false intimacy. We want to affirm a real relation in faith, now alive and deeply sensed in our faith, a true love for a fellow member of Christ.

The kiss of peace, the greeting, is a sign of caring and concern. It is, in fact, an affront if it does not reflect a reality. As I have said, in some Eucharists it is certainly not a problem. It is a joyous moment that tends to be prolonged. I remember attending an ordination at our cathedral. The kiss of peace went on and on as the one-hundred and fifty priests went around the sanctuary embracing each other and shaking hands heartily. And the vast congregation, having completed their mutual greetings, stood there smiling from ear to ear as they witnessed this great outpouring of affection among their priests.

Surprisingly enough when one drops into a church as a stranger, there is often a very cordial greeting. The local people seem eager to reach out, acknowledging that there is a bonding in Christ to be expressed.

The problem seems to be primarily in stable—parochial and religious —communities. Those gathered seem to know there could be more caring than there is. The greeting seems a sham. Should it then be omitted? No! Let it challenge us. It says what should be. Let us make it so. This certainly doesn't rule out differences among us. The Apostles seem to have had rows regularly and even started off the first Mass, the Last Supper, with one. It is time to let go of the differences and affirm that even in the midst of them there are deeper bonds—essentially we do care about each other's well-being.

The kiss of peace does not rule out a lack of intimacy, it doesn't rule out great numbers. There can still be a sense of oneness in a basic relationship, in a common quest, in a centering on the one Christ. We have experienced it at great charismatic gatherings. We have seen it among vast numbers at the Masses of Pope John Paul II. In these great throngs numbers were no problems. A lack of intimacy was no problem. We were together, children of one most loving Holy Father. There was focus. There was commitment. And it expressed itself in appropriate sharing and caring as we waited, as we celebrated, as we departed. Some of us couldn't help contrasting the joyful patience after the papal Mass, as the great throngs and the thousands of cars and buses took hours to depart for home, and the sad scenes that we have all experienced in small parochial parking lots as fifty cars jockey for one exit. We need to let the kiss of peace challenge us on an everyday basis to a life of sharing and caring in ever-widening circles—parish, church, world— otherwise Communion really has no meaning.

The Lord in his liturgy does want to challenge us. That is why we go immediately from an expression of peace and unity to one of fraction. The bread is broken. And we sing of a Lamb that was slain. We are graphically and conceptually reminded that the healing of our brokenness, our struggle toward unity and peace, comes out of a costly sacrifice.

The lamb was the most favored of sacrifices. Even at the gates of Eden it was pleasing to God as it was offered from Abel's pure heart. It was the symbol used in the saving of the chosen people from bondage, a symbol enshrined at the heart of their memorial liturgy, ever looking forward to the true Lamb, the symbol offered first at that supper which was to bring it to completion. After the lamb was divided and distributed and eaten, then Jesus took bread, unleavened bread; and breaking it, he distributed it—no longer a symbolic lamb, but the Lamb of God, who takes away the sin of the world. But still a breaking, still a sacrifice, still a cost.

The instruction in the missal insists that "the Eucharistic bread, even though unleavened, should be made in such a way that the priest can break it and distribute the parts to at least some of the faithful." It is sad that a certain indifference or convenience or laziness often wins out and no effort is made to have a solid piece of bread that can adequately fulfill its symbolic role. Communities depend on ritual and symbol to express together their deepest values and communion in them. Every family that is well-rooted and united has them. The Mass, the central ritual of the Christian community, the family of God's children, expresses the mystery that is at the very heart of our communion and life in a rich collection of symbolic elements and actions. One of the keys to a meaningful community Eucharist is the proper presentation of these symbols so that the community can really experience itself expressing what is profoundly important and meaningful to us in them. Carelessness in preparing the symbolic elements and in carrying out the symbolic acts will undermine all other efforts for successful liturgy, especially if this carelessness touches on the most central symbols, those which express the essence of the sacrificial meal.

COMMUNION

�֍ �֍ �֍

Shortly after the general restoration of Communion under two forms, both bread and wine, I had the joy of offering the Eucharist with my brother's family in their beautiful Long Island home. The eight children were gathered around the large dining-room table with mother, father, and grandmother. The littlest sat at the opposite end of the table, propped up on pillows, wide eyes fixed steadily on my every action. I had tried to prepare the family for what would be for them a new sharing in the body and blood of Christ. Today, after receiving a piece of the sacred bread, they would also drink from the sacred cup, as I had always done and as our Lord had done and had told his Apostles and all of us to do in those words I always repeated: *Take this, all of you, and drink from it*. It made sense to the children who were used to doing what they were told and especially to doing what God told them to do. With a little reflection, they might well have wondered why they hadn't been doing it all along and why they weren't doing it when they went to Mass in the parish church.

This day it was something new for them. This cup was special. They had seen how many of the adults struck their breasts, or bowed down, or made the sign of the cross when the priest held up the chalice. They saw how I held it up to them with reverential awe when we celebrated at that table. Today, for the first time, they were going to be allowed to hold it and taste its contents—the blood of Christ. Unfortunately, I omitted an important part of their preparation. Before their first Communion they had all had a chance to finger an unconsecrated host, examine it, try it out, eat it. Getting past the unfamiliarity of the form they were ready to concentrate on the reality. I did not think to do this with the chalice. The youngest communicants watched as first Dad, then Mom, then the older brothers and sisters received the blood of Christ. Things went fine, for all of them had tasted wine before. But then it came to Neil's turn. The strange burning liquid had never touched his lips before. As the burning sensation ran down into his stomach a most awful grimace clutched every inch of his usually angelic face. The older communicants, watching from under partially closed eyes, had all they could do to keep from bursting into laughter—including the celebrant. This unforgettable incident drove one lesson home: the importance of a complete and thorough preparation for liturgical changes.

I believe that it is precisely a failure in this respect that has—and I say it with a deep sadness—turned the very heart and center of all unity, Communion itself, into an occasion of discord and disunity. We poor sinful creatures have such a power to frustrate the most sublime and beautiful designs of the Almighty. May he have mercy on us.

Our Lord's part in this is so clear and simple. He took a big piece of unleavened bread and said: *Take this, all of you, and eat it; this is my body which will be given for you*; he broke it and gave it to his disciples. Then he took a cup of wine and said: *Take this, all of you, and drink from it, this is the cup of my blood, the blood of the new and everlasting covenant. It will be shed for you and for all so that sins may be forgiven*; and handed the cup to them. And each drank from it. Finally he said: *Do this in memory of me.* With things so simple and clear it is hard to see how we have gotten into such a fuss.

True, after some centuries problems did arise and practices did evolve. Probably one of the key factors was the heresy promoted in the fourth century by a man called Arius. He and his followers had an immense influence. He said Jesus was not fully God like his Father. And this man and his followers convinced almost the whole Church. Such a heresy had to be rejected with a resounding affirmation of Jesus' full divinity. The reaction was so strong that the Incarnation and Jesus' true humanness began to be lost sight of. Jesus-God became more and more awesome. The sinner, like a leper, was to keep his distance. A rail went up to mark off the holy place; in the East, even a wall with veiled entrances, like in the Jerusalem Temple. God was remote again, locked in his sanctuary, no longer a man among his people, on their roads, in their homes. The earliest Christian practice of taking the Eucharist home for daily Communion was discontinued. In church one approached the rail or the holy doors less and less frequently and then only after confessing and getting a spiritual father's permission. In the West one came to him on one's knees. No longer did the communicant dare to touch the sacred chalice or the sacred bread. The East resorted to a spoon. In the West the host was placed on the tongue. Sometimes it was dipped, but that passed, too, until the West had Communion only under the form of bread for all save the celebrant. Even the celebrant was restricted to touching the host with only two fingers, carefully purified. One seemed to forget that his whole hand was anointed. Indeed, the whole body of the Christian is anointed at baptism.

How far these exaggerated forms of reverence are from the familial celebration of the first Mass and the practice of Christian communities through the first centuries that produced so many saints and martyrs! God had become man to be close to men and women, especially sinners. He ate with them, he drank with them. He touched them wherever they hurt. And they reached out and touched him wherever they could. Children clambered all over him.

It is true, though, for whatever reasons, we are the heirs to two traditions. For eight centuries Communion was received in the hand; then it began to be popped into the mouth or placed on the protruding tongue. For nearly twelve centuries the sacred host was not received without the precious blood, but then in the West (and only in the West) it was given without the cup. Certainly the Lord is wholly present in the host placed on the tongue; the reality of Communion is complete even if the sacramental sign is incomplete. So it is quite right to allow mature Christians to make their own judgment as to whether it is better for them to follow the later custom rather than literally to obey the Lord.

Jesus, our Creator, knew well the persons he made. He knew the way apt signs would form our minds and hearts. He wanted us to know his intimate love for us, how he would care for us and sustain us until he brought us to the great celebration in heaven, which he called a banquet, where we would always enjoy the communion of his love. So he gave himself in the form of a sustaining meal and he served us the way one serves friends. He broke his own bread for them and shared his own cup—one could hardly have imagined a meal where one only ate and had nothing to drink! He did say we had to be little ones to enter the kingdom, but not babies who have the food placed in their mouths.

The sacramental sign is certainly filled out in our experience when we take and drink as the Lord said. All the senses are directly and intimately touched. As the cup is presented we are told directly: the blood of Christ —the blood of the New Covenant is indeed shed for us; it is being placed in our very hands. We see it in the sacred wine. The smell and taste is strong, the feel of warmth penetrates us deeply—all bespeak his presence, a deep communion in love. For most of us in the West wine is more than ordinary nourishment, it bespeaks something special, celebration. It is to be shared. There is something ominous about drinking alone. As we all drink from one cup we know Communion.

Intinction, of course, misses a lot of this symbolism; that is why the American bishops have discouraged it. They have encouraged having only one chalice or a flask on the altar, which can be distributed into other cups at the time of the fraction, to further bring out the unity and the sacrificial outpouring. It will take more ministers to share the cup with large parochial congregations. That is good. More active participation, more of the whole Church involved in its common priesthood.

That is also one of the benefits of receiving the sacred bread in one's hand. The recipient is more actively involved, is invited to be more conscious of his shared priesthood. We are all a royal priesthood, we who have been baptized into the priesthood of Christ, the great High Priest. The special ordination of some to particular ministries in the Church (deacons, priests, and bishops) the special consecration of some persons by vows (monks, nuns, and religious), does not mean all are not partakers in the priesthood of Christ and consecrated by baptism, just as getting married, becoming a sacrament of the love between Christ and his Church (this is what makes marriage, of itself a natural institution, to be a sacrament), doesn't mean the rest of us are not to foster and show forth this love-relation of the Church and Christ. In our diverse vocations we take upon ourselves particular responsibilities to show forth aspects of Christ and to fulfill the duties of his whole body in a way that stands out and encourages the whole Church. We receive special graces to do this in the sacraments or rites that initiate us into these vocations.

Historically, we have seen, it was a sense of reverence that caused the shift in the way the faithful responded to the sacrament, a reverence nurtured by fear rather than by love, that centered on self and one's sins rather than on God and his merciful Incarnation. Reverence remains one of the most often expressed reasons why some prefer to receive the sacred bread on the tongue rather than in the hand.

Certainly the tongue has not received any consecration over and beyond that received by the hand. Perhaps we are more conscious of the sins of the hand; they are more blatant: theft, masturbation, mistreating others. We do tend to be much more careless about sins of the tongue: lying, calumny, slander, detraction, cursing, swearing, taking God's name in vain. "The one who sins not with his tongue is a perfect one," says Saint James. I might paraphrase Saint Paul's "All have sinned and all need the mercy of God," saying all our members have sinned, and all need to be purified. Like the hemorrhaging woman, ritually unclean, we need to reach out and touch the Lord.

There is something beautifully humble and reverent about the way we take Communion in the hand. A good gesture symbolizes and creates an experience. Who hold out their hands? The humble, the dependent—children and beggars—those who long for something and desire it, and they hold out their hands as long as they can expect to receive or at least have some hope. Among the most poignant memories etched in my heart are those of the little ones in India who were both children and beggars. Their grimy little hands would reach up tirelessly, with desperate longing, clinging to hope as long as they could. How tragically the light faded from their eyes when finally they dropped their hands to their side empty.

We hold out our hands, humble, poor, needy, expecting, and receiving All. In the fourth century, the Christians of Jerusalem were told:

> When you approach, do not stick out your open hands or have your fingers spread out, but make your left hand into a throne for the right which shall receive the King and then cup your open hand and take the Body of Christ reciting the "Amen."

Christ comes to rest for a moment on the throne of our hands before entering the inner chamber of our being. It affords us a most precious moment of intimate reflection. All our senses come into play. We hear said to us directly, *The Body of Christ*; we see him in bread resting in our hand, we feel him; if the bread is what it should be we can even smell the wholesome nourishing odor of the bread of life. Desire quickly mounts to new peaks to "taste and see how sweet is the Lord."

Change is always difficult for all of us, especially as we get older. Our past experience has taught us. If we have received Communion one way for years we will have come to associate with it many good experiences. There is nothing in our own experience to assure us that the same good experiences, or even better ones, will be found in another way. The only way to discover that God can and does act in other ways is to try them and let him show us himself. If we have the testimony of others that it is so, it is worth the try.

THE MASS IS

I recently celebrated the silver jubilee of my ordination to the priesthood. Many wonderful friends gathered from far and near to join in the community celebration. Among them was a young priest friend from Washington who is an excellent dancer. I invited him to dance for us during the quiet time after Communion. Another priest wrote a beautiful musical piece entitled "In the Quiet Time." He would dance to this music.

It was a first for our community. We had never had anyone dance in our church before. Some of the brothers were apprehensive. As I sat in the president's chair behind the altar I rested quietly, gratefully in the Lord, forgetting about Bruce's dance until the gentle music stepped into our quiet. It actually fitted in so well that some never became aware of the dance. They continued to rest quietly in the Lord in the flow of the music. For others the graceful body that expressed the music in another dimension expressed the deepest movements of their souls magnificently and intensified them.

Afterward a brother told Bruce that he had gone to the liturgy set on not liking the dancing, but it had been one of the most beautiful things he had ever experienced. An old priest said that in his fifty years he had never seen a liturgical dance—he thought it was beautiful. These men opened themselves to a new experience and they were blessed by it.

The quiet time after Communion is very important. Some people complain that there is so much going on at Mass they can't pray anymore. The silent Mass is gone—and it should be. But silence in the Mass shouldn't be. The General Instruction in the missal says: "Silence at designated times is also a part of the celebration." At the opening of the celebration, as the president gathers the community, each one needs a moment to come to presence, perhaps a moment of examen and repentance, but always a moment of conversion, a turning from the scattering of many thoughts to a centering on God and the communal encounter with him. Each time the president says "Let us pray," he needs to allow the community to enter into prayer and he himself needs to share that prayer so that he can collect it all in the oration. After each reading and the homily the hearers need a quiet moment to assimilate what they have heard, otherwise it will be quickly lost.

When the offertory procession and song are complete it is well to leave the community a quiet freedom. The priest is performing some important symbolic acts: water flows into the chalice and mingles with the wine, incense embraces gifts and altar and rises noiselessly to heaven, water washes away the vestiges of contamination. A silent reflective perception of these can be powerful.

Immediately before Communion each is left to his or her own prayer while the celebrant prepares personally for his Communion and receives his Lord. In the Eastern Christian liturgies a veil is drawn at this time before the altar and a candle placed before it. It is a sacred moment which the community embraces in its silence, expecting the moment of its own Communion when the veil will be opened and the priest will come forth with the chalice: "With the fear of God, with faith and with love, draw near."

The importance and significance of each of these moments should be understood by the worshiping community. I think many have difficulty with the silence because it has never been explained to them, how much it is a part of the whole fabric of their communal worship, which must be true worship and prayer coming from the depths of the heart of each participant. The pause after Communion seems in many ways the most important one.

During the Communion service the community might well sing appropriate songs or respond to the choir's chant with some refrain. The communion service can be as active as a cocktail party, a tea, or a buffet dinner. There is much moving about as all go to receive the bread and the cup. It is a shared meal and there is a lot of participation as we pass things out and clean up. Some singing can focus things. But once all are served and things settle down it is almost natural for an awesome silence to descend on the community as each one rests deep within in the embrace of a God who is love. At this point the right music (almost any instrument or voice could be used here) or the quiet rhythmic movements of a dance might powerfully support a transcendent experience. It is an opportunity for some of the gifted members of the community to make their special contribution. Obviously it has to be a contribution in service or supporting a communal experience, not an attempt to shine for a moment and draw attention to oneself. It is a supporting role, supporting the focus of attention on the Presence, in himself or herself and in the community.

What about using recorded music? Some have a very strong adversion to "canned" music and would rather hear inferior local attempts, or nothing, than electronic reproductions. My own thinking on this has evolved. Not every community is graced with true talent. A real effort should be made to call forth what there is and cultivate it. But a good recording might support the prayerful state and the sense of presence and communion better than some ragged local effort.

Our worship, rich in tradition, embraces the here and now. New ministries have their import: proper monitoring of the public-address system, audio and video recording and transmission, photography—so many things that enhance and enlarge communal participation. Technology can reach out and bring in the contribution of other members of the body of Christ not present, contributions made at other times and places but all with our celebration in the "now" of God. *All things are ours, and we are Christ's.* We shouldn't hesitate to use anything that can fittingly and helpfully be used for our uplifting and his glory.

The use of recorded contributions should certainly not be allowed to squeeze out all local offerings or be an expression of a certain laziness. Recorded music should be chosen and prepared with as much care and effort as an actual performance. The presentation of the carefully chosen piece should be as perfect as possible: all equipment should be in place so that it can proceed without any awkward delays or noises. The contribution should quietly find its place without undue distraction.

The president is to bring all the power of this moment of deep communion together into a prayer that will reinforce it with God's enabling grace and send it forth. The missal, here as elsewhere, gives the priest guiding texts, but his prayer following the line of the text should flow out of the fullness of the moment and the communal experience. After the prayer he might even articulate this experience in a few words. It is an apt time for those announcements that call forth the community to translate some of the fullness of their experience into the life ahead. A special appeal to generosity for particular needs aptly finds its place here. Through our hard-earned money, the fruit of our lives, we can go forth to others in comforting and healing Christlike love. The collection could be gathered as the community goes out to active Christian participation in life.

The celebrant prays again for each: *The Lord be with you,* and he blesses them and sends them forth, one by one, two by two, family by family, but still an empowered community in the oneness of Christ. On special days there are special blessings. We have celebrated a particular mystery of God's love—an event of Christ's life or of his Church in her saints—and it is the grace of that particular event which the community is charged to bring forth out of their own fullness to the needy world.

Go, the Mass is. Ite, missa est. The old Latin dismissal (which can more properly be translated, "Go, it is the dismissal") was so important that it gave its name to the Liturgy: *missa*, Mass. This, we can hope, was not because the people were eager to be done with it and on their way (though from the way some act at the end of the Mass this is quite believable). This moment of dismissal gave its name to the whole because of its prime importance. It does sum up the whole and charges each one to take it—the whole infinitely empowering experience of Calvary and Communion—out into the world. We are sent, it is a mission, to make the passion of Christ healingly present in our world today. Our Lord said, *Judge a tree by its fruit.* If our participation in the liturgy does not bear fruit in our lives and the lives of others as we go forth into daily life then there is something radically wrong with the way we celebrate Eucharist.

The word Eucharist means thanksgiving. The silent moments after Communion are moments of thanksgiving, a thanksgiving more of complete responsive presence than of particular words—a complete "yes" to God and his love. The priest's prayer also is a prayer of thanksgiving but he prays that we may show our true gratitude not just in words, but with God's grace, by living out of the fullness of what we have received. The best way to show our gratitude is to use well what we have been given.

As Jesus stood on Olivet that Ascension Thursday he blessed his disciples and gave them his final charge. It was the end of that Mass, that passover mystery, the whole of his mission on this earth, and his charge was: Go and bring the Good News effectively to all. Through his priest he gives us the same charge as we complete our Mass. A seed has been planted in the Church and it is to burst forth in the world. The chaos that sometimes ensues in the parking lot may indeed seem like an eruption. But even as our gathering is sacramental, so should our going forth—going out of the door of the church, out of the parking lot—it should be sacramental. We don't have to wait until we are a block away or a mile away before we begin to bring beauty to the world in the loving, caring life of a Christian. On the front porch of the church, on the steps, or in the parking lot we can care, we can smile, we can say and do the compassionate and affirming thing. And then back home in the family, and through the week at our place of work, in stores, wherever we go. A particular examen for the week might well be to ask ourselves each evening as we close our day: How was what I received at the Eucharist shared today? Was I a sacrament of the love and compassionate care of Christ? If we can say yes, then the Mass is not just an event quickly celebrated in a church on Sunday morning. It is a reality that pervades our lives and our world. Then truly, the Mass is.

APPENDIX A

ANAPHORA OF SAINT BASIL

Let us stand well, let us stand in awe, let us be attentive to offer the holy oblation in peace.

A mercy of peace, a sacrifice of praise.

The grace of our Lord Jesus Christ and the love of God the Father and the fellowship of the Holy Spirit be with you all.

And with your spirit.

Let us lift up our hearts.

We have them lifted up to the Lord.

Let us give thanks to the Lord.

It is fitting and right to worship the Father, the Son and the Holy Spirit, Trinity one in substance and undivided.

O You who are Being, Master and Lord, God, almighty and adorable Father: it is truly fitting and right and worthy of the immensity of your holiness that we praise You, sing to You, bless You, adore You, give thanks to You, glorify You who alone are truly God; that we offer You a spiritual worship with a repentant heart and a humble spirit, for it is You who granted us the favor of knowing your truth. How could anyone tell your might and sing the praises You deserve, or describe all your marvels in all places and times, O Master of All, Lord of heaven and earth and of all creatures visible and invisible, who are enthroned upon a seat of glory, who plumb the depths, who are eternal, invisible, beyond comprehension and description and change, the Father of our Lord Jesus Christ the great God and Saviour, the object of our hope! For He is the Image of your goodness, the Seal bearing your perfect likeness, revealing You his Father through Himself; He is the living Word, the true God, the Wisdom from before all ages, the Life, the Sanctification, the Power, the True Light. By Him the Holy Spirit was made manifest, the Spirit of truth, the Gift of adoption, the Foretaste of the future inheritance, the First-fruits of eternal good, the life-giving Power, the Fountain of sanctification. Empowered by Him, every rational and intelligent creature sings eternally to your glory, for all are your servants. It is You the angels, archangels, thrones and dominations, the principalities and the virtues, the powers and the cherubim of many eyes adore; it is You the seraphim surround, one with six wings and the other with six wings; and with two wings they cover their faces, and with two their feet, and with two they fly, and they cry one to the other with tireless voice and perpetual praise: Singing, proclaiming, shouting the hymn of victory and saying:

Holy, Holy, Holy, Lord of Hosts: heaven and earth are filled with your glory. Hosanna in the highest. Blessed is he who comes in the name of the Lord. Hosanna in the highest.

With these blessed powers, O Master and Lover of Mankind, we sinners also cry and say: Verily holy are You, and all-holy, and there is no limit to the majesty of your holiness. Holy are You in all your deeds, for in righteousness and true judgment You have brought all things to pass for us: for having taken clay from the earth and having formed man, and honored him, O God, with your likeness, You placed him in a paradise of delight, and promised him immortality of life and the enjoyment of eternal goods in the keeping of your commandments. But when he disobeyed You, the true God and his Creator, and was deceived through the serpent's guile, and was subjected to death through his own transgression, in your just judgment, O God, You cast him forth from paradise into this world and turned him again to the earth whence he had been taken, and devised for him the salvation of regeneration which is in your Christ. For You did not turn away forever from your work, O gracious God, nor did You forget the work of your hands: You watched over us in many ways through the depth of your love; You sent forth prophets; You worked mighty signs through your saints who were pleasing to You in every age. You spoke through the mouths of your servants the prophets, promising the salvation to come; You gave us the Law to aid us; You set angels over us as our guardians. And when the fullness of time had come, You spoke to us by your Son through whom also You made the universe, who being the brightness of your glory and the express likeness of your Person, upholds everything by the power of his Word, and thought it no robbery to be equal to You his God and Father: but although He was God before creation, He was seen on earth and had his conversation among us; and being incarnate of the holy Virigin, emptied Himself and assumed the nature of a servant, and was found in the likeness of the body of our humiliation, that He might raise us to the likeness of his glory. For since it was by man that sin had entered the world, and death through sin, your only-begotten Son, He who was in your bosom, O You his God and Father, condescended to be born of a woman, the holy Mother of God and ever-virgin Mary—to be born under the Law in order to condemn sin in his flesh, that those who die in Adam might be quickened in your Christ: and having lived in this world and offered precepts of salvation and turned us away from the errors of idolatry, He brought us to the knowledge of You, the true God and Father, after purchasing us to Himself as a favored people, a royal priesthood, a holy nation. And after He had cleansed us with water and sanctified us with the Holy Spirit, He gave Himself up as a ransom to death by which we had been held for having been sold under sin; and through the cross, He went down into Hades that He might fulfill all things in Himself, and loosed the fangs of death. And He rose again the third day, preparing a way for the resurrection of all flesh from the dead because it was impossible that the Principle of life be held by corruption, and became the First-fruits of those who sleep, the Firstborn from among the dead so that in all things He might have primacy. And He ascended into heaven and was enthroned at the right hand of your Majesty on high, whence He shall come to render to every one his due. And He left us memorials of his salutary passion, these which we have brought about by his command. For being about to go forth to his willful and eternally memorable and life-giving death, on the night wherein He surrendered Himself for the life of the world, He took bread in his holy and spotless hands, presented it to You, his God and Father, gave thanks and blessed and sanctified and broke it, and gave it to his holy disciples and apostles, saying: Take, eat: this is my body, which is broken for you for the remission of sins.

    Amen.

Likewise, the chalice after He had supped, saying: Drink of this, all of you, this is my blood of the new testament, which is shed for you and for many for the remission of sins.

    Amen.

Do this in remembrance of Me, for as often as you eat this bread and drink this cup, you show forth my death and confess my resurrection. Remembering, therefore, this precept of salvation and everything that was done for our sake, the cross, the tomb, the resurrection on the third day, the ascension into heaven, the enthronement at the right hand, the second and glorious coming again: We offer You your own, from what is your own, in all and for the sake of all.

    We praise You, we bless You, we give thanks to You, Lord, and we pray to You, our God.

Therefore, most holy Lord, we also sinners and your unworthy servants called by You to serve at your holy altar, not by reason of our righteousness for we have done nothing good upon the earth, but by reason of your love and mercy which You have richly poured out upon us, we take courage and approach your holy table: offering to You the antitypes of the holy body and blood of your Christ, we beg You and implore You, in the good pleasure of your bounty, to make your Holy Spirit come down upon us and upon these present gifts offered to You, and to bless and sanctify them and offer them.

And make this bread the precious body of your Christ.

Amen.

And that which is in this chalice the precious blood of your Christ.

Amen.

Changing them by your Holy Spirit. Amen, amen, amen. So that, to those who partake of them, they may be for the cleansing of the soul, for the remission of sins, for the fellowship of your Holy Spirit, for the fullness of the kingdom of heaven, for intimate confidence in You, and not for judgment or condemnation.

Again, we offer You this spiritual worship for those resting in the faith, the forefathers, fathers, patriarchs, prophets, apostles, preachers, evangelists, martyrs, confessors, ascetics, and for every holy soul who has run the course in the faith. Especially for our all-holy, spotless, most highly blessed and glorious Lady the Mother of God and ever-virgin Mary.

In you, O woman full of grace, all creation exults, the hierarchy of angels together with the race of men: in you, sanctified Temple, spiritual Paradise, Glory of virgins of whom God took flesh—from whom our God who exists before the world, became a child! For He has made your womb his throne, making it more spacious than the heavens. In you, O Woman full of grace, all creation exults: glory to you!

For the holy prophet and forerunner John the Baptist, for the holy glorious and illustrious apostles, for holy N. whose memory we honor today, and for all your saints at whose supplication do You visit us, O God. And remember all those who have fallen asleep before in the hope of resurrection to eternal life. And give them rest where the light of your face keeps watch. Again, we pray You: remember, Lord all the Orthodox Bishops rightly dispensing the word of your truth, all the priests, the deacons in Christ and all the ranks of the clergy. Again, we pray You: remember, Lord, your holy, catholic and apostolic Church which is from one end of the earth to the other, and give her peace, for You purchased it to Yourself through the precious blood of your beloved Son; make firm this holy house until the consummation of all things. Remember, Lord, those who have offered You these holy gifts, and those for whom and through whom and on account of whom they offered them. Remember, Lord, those who bring forth fruit and do good work in your holy churches, and who care for the poor: reward them with your rich and heavenly blessings; bestow upon them heavenly gifts in exchange for the gifts of the earth, eternal gifts for those of time, incorruptible gifts for the corruptible. Remember, Lord, those who are in deserts and mountains and in the dens and caves of the earth. Remember, Lord, those who remain in virginity and continence and asceticism, and those who lead saintly lives in the world. Remember, Lord, our most faithful and pious public authorities which You have counted worthy to be appointed over this land: crown them with the armor of truth, with the armor of glory; cover their heads on the day of battle, strengthen their arm, exalt their right hand, establish their power. Subdue to them barbarous nations that delight in war; grant them deep peace that cannot be taken away; speak good things to their hearts for your Church and all your people, that within their peace we may lead a quiet and peaceable life in all godliness and honesty. Remember, Lord, all lawmakers and magistrates and our brethren in public office and in all Armed Forces: preserve the good in their goodness, and in your kindness, make the wicked become good. Remember, Lord the people present here, and those who are absent for reasonable causes; replenish our storehouses with all manner of goods; preserve our marriages in peace and harmony; nourish the babes, instruct the youths, console the elderly; comfort the feeble-minded, collect the scattered, bring back the wandering and unite them to your holy, catholic and apostolic Church. Free those who are bothered by unclean spirits; sail with those at sea, travel with the travelers, defend the widows, shield the orphans, preserve the prisoners, heal the sick. Remember, O God, those who stand before tribunals, and those in exile and in all kinds of tribulations and accidents, and all who need your great mercy; those who love us and those who hate us, and those who have begged us, unworthy though we be, to remember them in our prayers. Remember all your people, O Lord our God, and upon all pour forth your rich mercies, granting them everything they need for salvation. And those we have omitted through ignorance or forgetfulness or because of the multitude of their names, You Yourself remember, O God, who know the name and age of each, who have known each one from his mother's womb. For You, O Lord, are the Helper of the helpless, the Hope of the desperate, the Saviour of the tempest-tossed, the Harbor of voyagers, the Physician of the sick: become all things to all men, O You who know each man and his need, each house and its necessity. Preserve, O Lord, this city and every city and country place from plague, famine, earthquake, flood, fire, war, battle, invasion and riot. First, Lord, remember His Holiness John Paul, Pope of Rome, His Beatitude our Holy Patriarch, our Most Reverend Bishop. Preserve them as a blessing over your holy Churches in peace, safety, honor, health, long life, rightly dispensing the word of your truth.

Remember all men and women.

Remember, O Lord, all the Orthodox Bishops who rightly dispense the word of your truth. Remember also, Lord, my unworthiness, according to the multitude of your mercies; forgive my every transgression, deliberate and indeliberate, and do not withhold on account of my sins the grace of the Holy Spirit from the gifts offered here. Remember, O Lord, all the priests and the deacons in Christ, and let none of us who surround your holy table be put to shame. Look down upon us in your goodness, O Lord. Manifest Yourself to us in your rich mercies; grant us a healthful and agreeable climate; give showers to the earth that it may bring forth its fruits; bless with your goodness the crowning of the year; stay the schisms of Churches; restrain the raging of nations; by the might of your Holy Spirit, cast down rapidly the attempts of heresies; receive us all in your kingdom, making us children of light and sons of the day. Give us your peace and your love, O Lord our God, who have given us everything. And grant that with one mouth and one heart we may glorify and extol your most noble and magnificent name, of the Father and the Son and the Holy Spirit, now and always and for ever and ever.

Amen.

ANAPHORA OF SAINT MARK, EVANGELIST

Let us stand devoutly, for the gifts are about to be offered and heavenly glory is about to be revealed. The gates of heaven are open for the Holy Spirit to overshadow the Mysteries. May the love of God the Father, the grace of the Only-Begotten Son, and the unity and indwelling of the Holy Spirit be with you.

And also with you.

Let us all lift up our thoughts, our minds, and our hearts.

We lift them up to the Lord.

Let us confess the Lord with reverence, and worship Him with wonder.

It is proper to confess and worship Him.

It is proper to always confess You, mighty Lord. Angels praise You. Hosts worship You, and powers tremble before You. The assemblies of heaven unite to pay You tribute. Make us worthy to proclaim with them:

Holy, holy, holy, Lord God of hosts. Heaven and earth are full of Your glory. Hosanna in the highest. Blessed is He Who has come and will come in the name of the Lord. Hosanna in the highest.

O God, You are holy with Your Son and the Spirit. When we strayed from Your will, You sent Your Son to our aid. Through His saving passion, He restored us to the inheritance that was ours from the beginning. And by the sacred Blood He shed, He let us live again. Sin had no part with Him Who came to suffer for us. Before His passion, He took bread in His holy hands. He looked to heaven, gave thanks, blessed and broke, and said to His disciples: This is My Body. Take and eat of it for your forgiveness and for the forgiveness of all true believers unto everlasting life.

Amen.

Then He took the cup and mixed wine and water. He blessed and gave it to His disciples and said: This is My Blood of the new covenant. Take and drink of it for your forgiveness and for the forgiveness of all true believers unto everlasting life.

Amen.

Whenever You do this, You will proclaim My death and resurrection until I come.

O God, we commemorate Your death, we witness that You arose

from among the dead, and we await Your return. May Your mercy
come upon all of us.

O Lord God, we remember Your saving passion, Your resurrection, and
Your ascension. Because of Your plan of salvation, Your Church renews
Your saving action by offering this pure sacrifice as we say:

Have mercy on us, almighty God, have mercy.

We Your servants have received Your grace, and we give You thanks.

We praise You, we bless You, we adore You, we acknowledge and
ask of You: Have mercy on us, O Lord, and hear us.

How awesome is this moment! The Holy Spirit will descend to sanctify
these Mysteries.

O Lord, have mercy and hear us. Send forth Your Holy Spirit, equal to
You and the Son, that He may make us worthy ministers of this divine service. Hear me, O Lord; hear me, O Lord; hear me, O Lord.

Lord have mercy, Lord have mercy, Lord have mercy.

While blessing and sanctifying, may He make this bread the Body of
Christ our God.

Amen.

And this cup the Blood of Christ our God.

Amen.

May these holy Mysteries forgive our sins and cause us to stand with confidence before Your judgment seat. May they be for the help and upbuild-
ing of the holy Church, and keep her children from sin.

Amen.

O Lord, establish Your Church in peace and good order. Visit her bishops
with the wisdom of overseers, her priests with the fortitude of leaders,
and her deacons with the reverence of holy ministers. We remember in
particular our holy fathers, John Paul, the Pope of Rome, our Patriarch
of Antioch, and our Bishop.

Lord have mercy.

Remember those who share in this divine sacrifice. Heal their weakness,
free them from fear, and strengthen them in faith.

Lord have mercy.

Return those who have strayed from Your flock. Comfort travelers and
welcome strangers. Guide the religious communities, for You help those
in need.

Lord have mercy.

We remember at Your heavenly altar the holy, ever-Virgin, Mother of
God, Mary, John the Baptizer, Mark the evangelist, and all prophets,
apostles and martyrs. We recall Peter, Ignatius, and all those who have
suffered for Your holy Church.

Lord have mercy.

Remember those You have called from this life. Forgive them, for there is no one without sin except Your Son, our Lord Jesus Christ. Through Him we hope to find mercy and forgiveness.

Grant rest, O Lord, to the faithful departed.

O Lord, forgive us and allow us to depart this life free of guilt, that we may stand confidently before You. In the world to come we will offer You praise and thanksgiving now and forever.

As it was, is now and shall be forever. Amen.

ANAPHORA OF THOMAS THE APOSTLE

Let us stand devoutly.

In Your mercy, O Lord.

May the love of God the Father, and the grace of the Only-Begotten Son, and the unity and indwelling of the Holy Spirit be with you.

And also with you.

Let us raise our thoughts, our minds and our hearts.

They are raised to You, O Lord.

Let us praise and worship the Lord.

It is right and proper.

O Lord, You are awesome and praiseworthy in heaven and on earth. The ranks of the spiritual assembly who dwell in the Holy of Holies stand before You and adore Your honor. Without interruption, they call out:

Holy, Holy, Holy Lord, God of Hosts, Heaven and earth are full of your glory, Hosanna in the Highest. Blessed is He Who has come and will come in the Name of the Lord. Hosanna in the Highest.

In Your mercy, O Lord God the Father, You dealt with us in a fitting way through Your plan of salvation. You sent Your Only-Begotten Son, and He was joined to us in everything but sin for the redemption of life. He united Himself to the form of a slave so that He might complete the things of our salvation which were yet to come. He took bread, blessed, sanctified and broke and gave it to His Apostles saying: Take and eat, this is My Body. And when you do so, believe and confirm that you are eating My Body in memory of My death until I come again.

We remember Your Death, O Lord!

He took wine, blessed, sanctified and gave it to His Apostles saying: Take and drink, this is My Blood, the Blood of the New Covenant. And when you do so believe and confirm that you are drinking My Blood in memory of My death until I come again.

We proclaim Your Resurrection!

We also remember all those things which You endured O Word-God. From Your birth and baptism, to Your burial and Resurrection, to Your Ascension and sitting at the right hand of the Majesty of God the Father, and now we await Your powerful return. Your Church and flock implore You and Your Father saying:

Have mercy on us, Almighty God.

We Your servants, remember Your many graces and we thank You for them.

We praise You and we bless You. Have mercy on us, O Lord.

How awesome and powerful is this moment. For the Holy Spirit of God will descend upon us and upon these Mysteries. O God the Father, send now the grace of Your Holy Spirit, Who proceeds from You and Who is equal to You in Being and to Your Only-Begotten Son, that He may come and rest upon us and sanctify these Mysteries and make them perfect. Hear me, O Lord! Hear me, O Lord! Hear me, O Lord!

Lord, have mercy! Lord, have mercy! Lord, have mercy!

Giver of gifts, come to make this bread the Body of Christ our God, for the remission of faults, the forgiveness of sins, and the eternal life of those who receive it.

Amen.

And make this cup the Blood of Christ our God, for the remission of faults, the forgiveness of sins, and the eternal life of those who receive it.

Amen.

Through the acceptance of these Mysteries may we become sharers with You and may we be filled with that confidence which comes from You. We offer You praises, now and forever.

Amen.

O Lord, accept our offerings for tranquility among governments; for a blessing on this year, and for those who have any need.

Lord, answer us!

Send Your invisible gifts upon Your inheritance and all Your people. Remember those united with us and those known to You, who share in these offerings.

Lord, answer us!

O Lord, by the gifts of the Holy Spirit bestow Your constant assistance upon the pastors and the overseers, who guide Your flock. With the Gospel of Your Son, direct Your Church.

Lord, answer us!

O Lord, remember those who are persecuted for Your Holy Name. Remember, in particular, the Mother of the Lord of Saints, along with Maron and all the Saints, who have pleased You from one generation to another.

Lord, answer us!

O Lord, grant rest to our fathers, brothers and leaders, with all who have died professing the true faith. Entrust their spirit through our prayers to the mansions of rest. Likewise, be pleased with us, for we have the assurances of Your Son, through Whom ever new we hope.

Grant rest, O Lord, to the faithful departed.

O Lord, lead us all by Your unapproachable light. Unite us by Your benevolent power and establish us at Your right side with Your chosen ones, so that, as in this service, so also in all things, Your most honored Name may be glorified and praised with that of Your Beloved Son and Your Holy Spirit, now and forever.

As it was, is now and ever shall be. Amen.

ANAPHORA OF THE TWELVE APOSTLES

The Lord be with you all.
With your spirit.
Give thanks unto our God.
It is right, it is meet.
Lift up your hearts.
We have lifted them unto the Lord our God.
We give You thanks, O Lord, in Your beloved Son, our Lord Jesus, Whom in the last days You did send to us, Your Son, the Savior and Redeemer, the Angel of Your counsel, Who is the Word from You, and through Whom You made all things by Your will.

O Holy Trinity, Father and Son and Holy Spirit, bless them, Your people, Christians beloved and earthly, bless and send upon us the grace of the Holy Spirit, and make the doors of Your holy Church to open to us in Your mercy and in faithfulness; and perfect us in the faith of holiness unto the last breath.

O my Lord Jesus Christ, visit the sick of Your people, and heal them, and guard our fathers and our brothers who have gone forth and are traveling abroad, and bring them back to their dwelling in peace and in health.

Bless the airs of heaven and the rains and the fruit of the earth of this year according to Your grace, and make joy and gladness perpetual on the face of the earth, and establish for us Your peace.

Turn the heart of mighty kings to deal kindly with us always. Give favor to the elders of Your holy Church all the time to all, to each by their several names in the presence of powerful kings; our God lift them up.

And rest the souls of our fathers and our brothers and our sisters, who have fallen asleep and gained their rest in the true faith.

And bless those who occupy themselves with the incense and oblation, and the coins and the oil and the chrism, and the veils and the books of the lessons of the sanctuary, and the vessels of the sanctuary, that Christ our God bring them to the heavenly Jerusalem.

And all those who are assembled with us to entreat for mercy; Christ, our God, be propitious unto them, and all those who give alms before Your awful and terrible throne, and receive them.

And lift up every straitened soul, and those who are bound in chains, and those who are in exile and captivity and those who are held, that we may remember them in the time of our prayer, and we beseech You remember them in Your heavenly Kingdom; and drive away from me sin; remember me Your work.

O Lord, save Your people and bless Your heritage, govern them and lift them up for ever.

Have mercy on them, O Lord, and be propitious to our archpopes, bishops, presbyters, and deacons, and all Your Christian people.

For us and for them all, rest their souls and be propitious unto them, You who sent Your Son from heaven unto the bosom of the Virgin. He was carried in the womb, was made flesh, and his birth was revealed of the Holy Spirit.

Unto You before whom stand a thousand thousands, and ten thousand times ten thousand, the holy angels and Your honorable creatures that have six wings, the seraphim and the cherubim.

With two of their wings they cover their face, with two of their wings they cover their feet, and with two of their wings they fly from end to end of the world.

Continually, therefore, as they all hallow You and praise, with all those who hallow You and praise You, receive our hallowing also which we utter unto You:

> *Holy, Holy, Holy Lord of Sabaoth, the heavens and the earth are wholly full of the holiness of Your glory.*

The heavens and the earth are full of the holiness of Your glory, O our Lord and our God and our Savior Jesus Christ, Your only Son. He came and was born of the Virgin that he might fulfill Your will and make a people for You.

> *Remember us, O Lord, in Your kingdom: remember us, O Lord, O master, in Your kingdom; remember us, O Lord, in Your kingdom, as You remembered the thief on the right when You were on the tree of the holy cross.*

He stretched out his hands to the passion, suffering to save the sufferers who trust in him; who was delivered of his own will to the passion, that he might abolish death and burst the bond of Satan and trample on Sheol and lead forth our saints, establishing a covenant which shall make known his resurrection.

He took bread.

> *We believe that this is in truth; we believe.*

He looked up to heaven toward You, toward his Father; he gave thanks.

He blessed and broke, and he gave to his disciples and he said to them: Take, eat, this bread is my body which is broken for you for the forgiveness of sins.

> *Amen, Amen, Amen, we believe and confess, we praise You, our Lord and our God, that this is true we believe.*

And likewise also the cup, giving thanks, he blessed it and hallowed it, and he gave it to his disciples, and he said to them: Take, drink, this cup is my blood which is shed for you and for many.

Amen, Amen, Amen, we believe and we confess.

And as often as you do this, make a memorial of me.

We show Your death, O Lord, and Your holy resurrection; we believe Your ascension; and Your coming again; we praise You and confess You; we supplicate You and confess You, our Lord and our God.

Now also, Lord, remembering Your death and Your resurrection, we confess You and offer unto You this bread and this cup, giving thanks unto You; and thereby You have made us meet to stand before You and do Your priestly service. We pray You, O Lord, and beseech You, that You would send Your Holy Spirit and power upon this bread and upon this cup. May he make it body and blood of our Lord and our God and our Savior Jesus Christ for ever and ever.

Amen; O Lord have mercy upon us, O Lord have mercy upon us, and be propitious unto us.

With all our hearts we beseech the Lord our God, that he vouchsafe unto us the good communion of the Holy Spirit.

As it was, is, and shall be unto generations of generations world without end.

Truly the body and blood even to his hands and feet.

Give it altogether unto all those who take of it, that it be unto them for sanctification and for fulfilling with the Holy Spirit, and for confirming true faith, that they may hallow and praise Your beloved Son, Jesus Christ, with the Holy Spirit.

Amen. Grant us to be united in Your Holy Spirit, and heal us by this presphora, that we may live in You for ever world without end. Blessed be the name of the Lord, and let the name of his glory be blessed. So be it; so be it; blessed; so be it.

APPENDIX B

A NEW EUCHARISTIC LITURGY FROM INDIA

(*The celebrant introduces the Mass and greets the community:*)

Fullness there, fullness here, from fullness fullness proceeds. Once fullness has proceeded from fullness, fullness remains.

(PURIFICATION RITE)

(*The celebrant washes his hands and sprinkles some water on the people saying:*)

As our body is made clean by this water,
may our soul be made spotless by your grace.

(*The celebrant invites all to review their life. Then all pray:*)

Praise to the refuge of all
Praise to the most merciful
Praise to him who is eternal purity
Praise to the spotless one
Praise to the destroyer of sin
Praise to the protector of the just
Praise to the remover of ignorance.

(*The celebrant, holding the right hand up, facing the people, pronounces the following formula of absolution:*)

May the God of peace who brought from the dead our Lord Jesus,
the great shepherd of the sheep, by the blood of the eternal covenant,
equip you with everything good, that you may do his will,
working in you that which is pleasing in his sight,
through Jesus Christ to whom be glory for ever and ever. Amen.

(*All exchange the sign of peace.*
The lighting of the lamp: Celebrant lights the big lamp with the arati lamp.)

Praise to the divine light
Praise to the true light
Praise to the light of life

> *Praise to the light of the world*
> *Praise to the light of the self*
> *Praise to the inner light.*

Eternal light, shining beyond the heavens,
radiant sun, illuminating all regions, above, below and across,
true light enlightening every man coming into the world,
dispel the darkness of our hearts
and enlighten us with the splendor of your glory.

> *Your word is a lamp for our steps*
> *a light on our path.*

(The celebrant touches the flame with the tips of his fingers and then brings his fingers to his eyes. All turn to the light and perform the same gesture.)

(LITURGY OF THE WORD)
(Homage is paid to the books with light and incense. During the readings, the people remain with open hands and the palms turned upwards resting on their knees.
The celebrant blesses the readers saying:)

> May he who quickens the intellect and kindles the heart strengthen
> you with his power to proclaim the saving word.

(The Bible is read. Followed by a short silent meditation.
The Gospel is read. There follows the homily. This is followed by a silent reflection.
The celebrant invites the community to formulate their intentions. He concludes the prayer of the faithful.
The celebrant takes the dish of eight flowers as he says:)

> Father, send down your Spirit upon these offerings,
> the symbols of our self-gift to you.
> May we be pleasing in your sight.
> May we be united with the sacrifice of your Son.

(The celebrant places the eight flowers on the tray with the bread and wine in the eight directions, saying each time one of the following attributes of Jesus Christ:)

> Jesus, the Lord
> Jesus, the Son of God
> Jesus, the Son of Mary
> Jesus, the God-man
> Jesus, the true person
> Jesus, the anointed one
> Jesus, the true teacher
> Jesus, the savior.

(The celebrant making an offering with light and incense over the offerings, continues:)

To whom with you and the Holy Spirit be honor and glory now and forever. Amen.

(EUCHARISTIC PRAYER)

May your Holy Spirit, O God, enlighten our minds and open our lips,
that we may sing the wonders of your love!
    Help us, Spirit Divine, to proclaim God's mercy!
Let us praise and thank the Lord, our God,
whose majesty pervades the universe!
    Great is his name and worthy of praise!
Let us celebrate the glory of the Lord
whose splendor shines in the depths of our hearts.
    Glory to him in whom we have our being!
O supreme Lord of the Universe,
You fill and sustain everything around us.
You are the Ancient of Days
who turned, with the touch of your hand,
chaos into order, darkness into light.
Deep and wonderful, the mysteries of your creation.
You formed us in your own image,
entrusted the earth to our care,
and called us to share
in your own being, your own knowledge, your own bliss.
    Praise to the One who is Being, knowledge, bliss.
    Praise to the eternal reality.
    Praise to the fullness of all perfections.
Father most kind and merciful
you want all to reach the shores of salvation.
You reveal yourself to all
who search for you with a sincere heart.
You are the Power almighty adored as Presence hidden in nature
the Light that shines bright in the hearts of all who seek you
through knowledge and love, sacrifice and detachment.
You chose for yourself a people and made with them a lasting covenant.
Despite their infidelity, you were true to your promise,
and taught them to long for the day of the Savior
the day of peace and salvation for all.
    Praise to the expectation of the Nations,
    Praise to the promised one of Israel,
    Praise to him who comes in the name of the Lord.

O God invisible,
at the favorable time you were pleased to become visible to us.
Your Word, your only begotten Son,
took on our human condition and was born of the Virgin Mary.
As Supreme Teacher and Master,
he imparted the words of eternal life
to the poor and humble of heart.
He went about doing good.
When his hour had come,
of his own accord he laid down his life as a sacrifice for our sin.
Raised from the dead by you, Father, he became for us the source of life
and sent the Holy Spirit to fill the world with joy and peace.
Now we pray you, Father, send this same Spirit to fill these gifts of
bread and wine with his divine power,
and to make present among us the great mystery of our salvation.
  Come, O Spirit Supreme,
  Come, O Spirit all-holy
  Come, O Spirit who fill the universe.
At the Supper which he shared with his disciples,
your Son, Jesus Christ, took bread in his sacred hands,
gave you praise and thanks,
broke the bread and gave it to his disciples, saying:
Take this all of you, and eat it:
This is my body
which will be given up for you.
Do this to celebrate the memorial of me.
  Amen.
In the same way after supper,
he took the cup.
Again he gave you praise and thanks,
gave the cup to his disciples, saying:
Take this, all of you, and drink from it:
This is the cup of my blood,
the blood of the new and everlasting covenant.
It will be shed for you and for all
so that sins may be forgiven.
Do this to celebrate the memorial of me.
  Amen.
And so, Father, in gratitude we celebrate the memorial
of the obedient death of your Son,
of his glorious resurrection from the dead.
the triumphant ascension into heaven.

and his outpouring of the Spirit in whom the Church is born.
While we offer you his unique and holy sacrifice
we await his return in glory.
When he comes he will gather up the fruits of redemption,
hold them together in his fullness
and place them at your feet.

> *We announce your death*
> *and proclaim your resurrection, Lord Jesus;*
> *gather all your people into your kingdom when you come in glory.*

Merciful Father, bring together all your people in the Holy Spirit;
help them live in unity and fellowship with John Paul, our Pope,
our Bishop, the patriarchs, bishops and pastors of all the Churches.
Bless all our brethren who are not present at this Eucharist.

Bless all the efforts of all those who labor
to build a world, where the poor and hungry will have their fill,
where all peoples will live in harmony,
where justice and peace, unity and love will reign.

Grant to all the departed a share in your bliss.
Welcome them in your Kingdom,
where, Mary, the Virgin Mother of God,
the Apostles and Martyrs, the Saints of all lands and ages,
unceasingly pray for us and help us share in the riches
of your Son, our Lord Jesus Christ.

Loving Father, send down your Spirit,
the fullness of your bliss,
fill with joy and peace all of us
who share in the Body and Blood of Christ,
that we may be one in him,
and manifest our unity in loving service.
May he be the pledge of our resurrection
and lead us in hope to the shore of eternal life
with all the just in the Kingdom of Heaven.

In the Oneness of the Supreme Spirit,
through Christ who unites all things in his fullness,
we and the whole creation give to you,
God of all, Father of all,
honor and glory, thanks and praise,
worship and adoration,
now and in every age, for ever and ever.

Amen. You are the Fullness of Reality,
One without a second,
Being, Knowledge, Bliss!

(COMMUNION RITE)
(The celebrant says a few words of introduction to the communion rite.
Then this prayer:)

This is the Bread that came down from Heaven;
whoever eats this Bread will never die.
This is the cup of immortal nectar;
whoever drinks of this cup will live forever.
For the Lord says, "He will have eternal Life,
and I will raise him up on the last day."
Do you believe this?
Yes, Lord, we believe,
for you have the words of eternal Life.

(Then the celebrant invites the people to recite the 'Lord's Prayer.'
All recite with folded hands:)

Our Father in heaven,
holy be your name,
your kingdom come,
your will be done,
on earth as in heaven.
Give us today our daily bread.
Forgive us our sins
as we forgive those who sin against us.
Do not bring us to the test
but deliver us from evil.
For the kingdom, the power and the glory are yours, now and
     forever. Amen.

(The celebrant breaks the bread for communion saying:)

The cup of blessing which we bless is the communion with the blood
of Christ. The bread which we break is the communion with the
body of Christ.
Because there is one bread, we who are many are one body, for we
all partake of the one bread.

(Then the celebrant invites the congregation to partake of the sacred
meal, saying:)

My feast is ready, says the Lord;
brothers and sisters, let us joyfully share in his banquet.

(After all have received communion, a short pause is observed, followed
by chanting.

This leads to complete silence.
Prayer.)

(CONCLUDING RITE)
(*The celebrant addresses a few parting words, inspiring the community with a sense of mission. Then he imparts the solemn blessing, saying:*)
May God, beyond all name and form, share with you his glory beyond measure, and make you enter into the mystery of his presence.
Amen.
May God who became manifest in Jesus Christ enlighten your minds, strengthen your wills and fill your hearts with love.
Amen.
May God, the indweller in the cave of your hearts, animate you with his life.
Amen.
And may the grace of our Lord Jesus Christ, and the love of God, and the fellowship of the Holy Spirit be with you all.
Amen.
(*Concluding hymn*)